# MAGICAL TOUR OF CHINA

## 奇妙 中国 游

### VOLUME 1
### 第 一 册

www.BetterChinese.com

# MAGICAL TOUR OF CHINA

Magical Tour of China Student Textbook - Volume 1
Simplified Chinese Characters

**Copyright © 2011 Better World Ltd.**

All rights reserved. No part of this publication may be adapted, reproduced, stored in a retrieval system or transmitted in any form or by any means, electronic, mechanical, photocopying, recording, or otherwise without permission from the publisher.

Founder: Li-hsiang Yu 虞丽翔
Publisher: Chi-kuo Shen 沈启国
Illustrations by Better World Ltd.
Published by Better World Ltd.
3 4 5 XLA 18 17 16

P. O. Box 695
Palo Alto, CA 94302, USA
Tel: +1-650-384-0902
Email: usa@betterchinese.com
Web: www.BetterChinese.com

Use this product with our Online Learning System at www.BetterChinese.com.

ISBN-13: 978-962-978-166-8
ISBN-10: 962-978-166-2

# 目录
## Contents

| | | |
|---|---|---|
| 第一课 | 我们要去中国 | 1 |
| Chapter 1 | We Are Going To China | |
| 第二课 | 集合 | 16 |
| Chapter 2 | The Group Gathers | |
| 第三课 | Cola 就是可乐 | 30 |
| Chapter 3 | Cola Is *Kele* | |
| 第四课 | 北京的车真多 | 43 |
| Chapter 4 | Beijing Has So Many Cars | |
| 第五课 | 见到爷爷奶奶 | 58 |
| Chapter 5 | Meeting Grandpa and Grandma | |
| 第六课 | 水饺还是睡觉？ | 71 |
| Chapter 6 | *Shuǐjiǎo* or *Shuìjiào*? | |
| 第七课 | 姑妈还是姨妈？ | 85 |
| Chapter 7 | Paternal Auntie or Maternal Auntie? | |
| 第八课 | 哪里，哪里 | 98 |
| Chapter 8 | *Nali, Nali* | |
| 第九课 | 吃北京烤鸭 | 113 |
| Chapter 9 | Having Beijing Duck | |

# 中国历代年表
## Chronology of Chinese History

| | |
|---|---|
| 公元前2070年 (2070 B.C.) | 夏朝 Xia Dynasty |
| 公元前1600年 (1600 B.C.) | 商朝 Shang Dynasty |
| 公元前1046年 (1046 B.C.) | 西周 Western Zhou Dynasty |
| 公元前770年 (770 B.C.) | 东周 Eastern Zhou Dynasty |
| 公元前221年 (221 B.C.) | 秦朝 Qin Dynasty |
| 公元前206年 (206 B.C.) | 西汉 Western Han Dynasty |
| 公元25年 (A.D.25) | 东汉 Eastern Han Dynasty |
| 公元220年 (A.D.220) | 三国 Three Kingdoms |
| 公元265年 (A.D.265) | 晋朝 Jin Dynasty |
| 公元420年 (A.D.420) | 南北朝 Southern and Northern Dynasty |
| 公元581年 (A.D.581) | 隋朝 Sui Dynasty |
| 公元618年 (A.D.618) | 唐朝 Tang Dynasty |
| 公元907年 (A.D.907) | 五代 Five Dynasties |
| 公元960年 (A.D.960) | 北宋 Northern Song Dynasty |
| 公元1127年 (A.D.1127) | 南宋 Southern Song Dynasty |
| 公元1206年 (A.D.1206) | 元朝 Yuan Dynasty |
| 公元1368年 (A.D.1368) | 明朝 Ming Dynasty |
| 公元1616年 (A.D.1616) | 清朝 Qing Dynasty |
| 公元1912年 (A.D.1912) | 中华民国 Republic of China |
| 公元1949年 (A.D.1949) | 中华人民共和国 People's Republic of China |

# 第一集
# 我们要去中国

Chapter 1
We Are Going To China

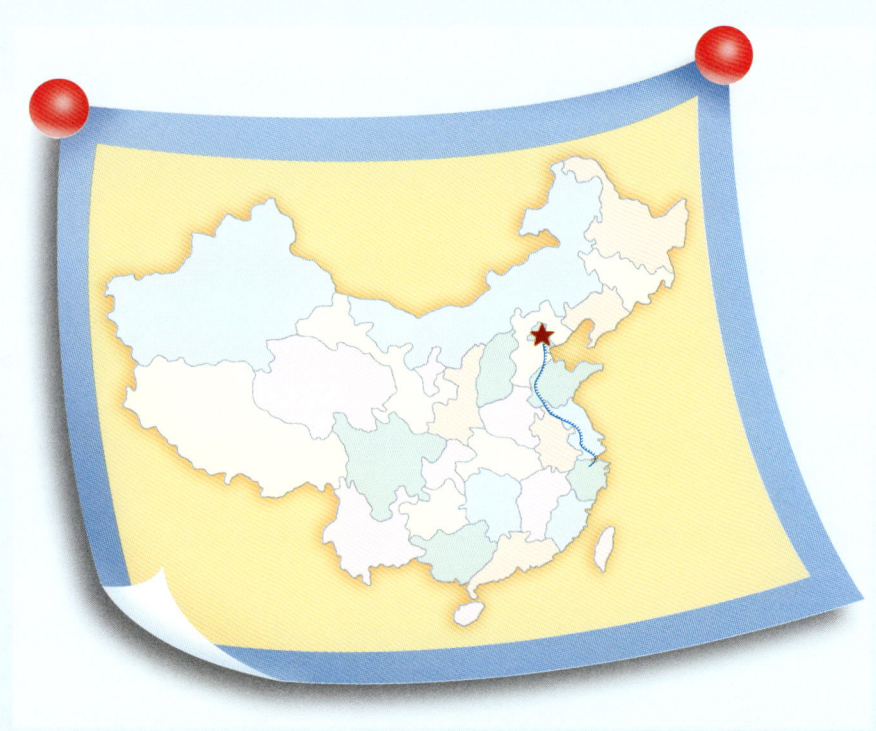

# 人物介绍

王家 WANG Family:
父母是第一代美国华人。
父亲：王大力
母亲：李美兰
儿子：王小龙
女儿：王小凤

史家 Smith Family:
父亲是欧洲后裔，母亲来自台湾。
父　亲：Mike
母　亲：Linda
大儿子：Jason
小儿子：David

张家 ZHANG Family:
父亲是华人，母亲是欧洲后裔。
父　亲：张华
母　亲：Mary
大女儿：Joy 张吉祥
小女儿：Ruby 张如意

# 第一集　我们要去中国
······ We Are Going To China

小龙，小凤，告诉你们一个好消息！我们要去中国旅行了！

真的吗？什么时候？

复活节假期，就是下个月。

妈妈，为什么要去中国？中国好玩吗？

当然了，你们可以见到爷爷奶奶，参观很多古迹，

吃地道的中国菜，看可爱的熊猫，和中国小朋友一起玩...你们的中文会进步哦！

除了我们家，还有张叔叔一家，Joy，Ruby 都会去。

我的朋友 Smith 一家也去，你们一路上都有朋友。

太棒了！

Jason, David! 下个月我们要去中国旅行了！

太棒了！我们是不是能看到长城？

Peking Duck! Peking Duck...

MAGICAL TOUR OF CHINA
奇妙中国游

# 第一集　我们要去中国
## ······ We Are Going To China

## 课文 Text

# 第一集 我们要去中国

王小龙家——

王大力：小龙，小凤，告诉你们一个好消息！我们要去中国旅行了！
小　龙：真的吗？什么时候？
王大力：复活节假期，就是下个月。
小　凤：妈妈，为什么要去中国？中国好玩吗？
李美兰：当然了，你们可以见到爷爷奶奶，参观很多古迹，吃地道的中国菜，看可爱的熊猫，和中国小朋友一起玩...你们的中文会进步哦！
王大力：除了我们家，还有张叔叔一家，Joy, Ruby 都会去。
李美兰：我的朋友 Smith 一家也去，你们一路上都有朋友。
小　龙：太棒了！

Smith家——

Linda: Jason, David! 下个月我们要去中国旅行了！
Jason: 太棒了！我们是不是能看到长城？
David: Peking Duck! Peking Duck...
Linda: 孩子们，听着：在中国你们只能说中文！
David: 噢！不！
Mike: Do I have to speak Chinese?
Linda: 当然。
Mike: "你好"、"再见"、"我爱你"。
Linda: 你可以慢慢学。你最好给你的儿子们做个好榜样。看你是不是真的爱我。

Joy家——

张　华：你们要带的东西准备好了吗？
Joy: 妈妈和我已经准备好了，可是 Ruby 还在忙。
张　华：Ruby, 你在找什么？
Ruby: 我想带我的芭比，还有我喜欢的饼干。
张　华：Ruby, 我们是去中国，不是去露营。在中国也可以买到你喜欢的饼干。
Ruby: 中国有麦当劳吗？
张　华：当然有！中国还有好多你想不到的好东西呢。你一定会玩得很开心的！

 生字词 Vocabulary

| | | |
|---|---|---|
| 凤 | fèng | phoenix |
| 告诉 | gào su | to tell |
| 好消息 | hǎo xiāo xi | good news |
| 旅行 | lǚ xíng | to travel |
| 复活节 | fù huó jié | Easter |
| 当然 | dāng rán | certainly, of course |
| 地道 | dì dào | authentic |
| 进步 | jìn bù | (to make) progress |
| 叔叔 | shū shu | uncle (father's younger brother), a courteous way of addressing an older man |
| 一路上 | yí lù shang | along the way |
| 太棒了 | tài bàng le | great, wonderful |
| 孩子 | hái zi | kid, child |
| 着 | zhe | [a grammatical word signifying a continued action] |
| 噢 | ò | oh [an exclamation] |
| 慢慢 | màn mān | slowly |
| 儿子 | ér zi | son |
| 榜样 | bǎng yàng | example, model |
| 准备 | zhǔn bèi | to prepare |
| 已经 | yǐ jīng | already |
| 忙 | máng | busy |
| 芭比 | bā bǐ | Barbie |
| 露营 | lù yíng | camping |
| 麦当劳 | mài dāng láo | McDonald's |
| 开心 | kāi xīn | happy, to have a good time |

你要去哪里？

我要去中国.

 语法 Grammar

## 要

① will, be going to

要去中国了，小龙特别高兴。
Xiaolong is very happy because he is going to China.

冬天来了，要下雪了。
Winter is coming, it's going to snow.

② to want

明天咱们出去玩儿，你们要带什么东西？
Tomorrow we are going out, what do you want to take?

你要喝什么？我要可乐。
What do you want to drink? I want cola.

## 看

① to see, to watch

她要去动物园看可爱的熊猫。
She will go to the zoo to see cute pandas.

小龙和小凤都喜欢看电影。
Both Xiaolong and Xiaofeng like to watch movies.

② to consider, to judge

我看这是个好办法。
I think it's a great idea.

我看他是个很好的人。
I think he is a nice man.

## 一

① 一家人: the same family

我们是一家人。
We are from the same family.

我们一家人寒假要去滑雪。
Our family will go skiing for winter vacation.

② 一路上: along the way. It is usually followed by 都 (all).

一路上我们都有朋友在一起。
We have friends all along the way.

小龙一路上都没有说话。
Xiaolong said nothing the whole way.

③ 一下子: In a short while; at once; all of a sudden. You can also say 一下。

这个故事很容易，我一下子就记住了。
The story is very simple, so I remembered it at once.

请等一下。
Please wait for a little.

## 练习例句　Sample exercises

（一）Use "一" to express "as a whole".

◆ 例句：放假了，我们开车出去玩儿，可是一路上都堵车。

1. 杯子掉到地上，弄得一_____都是水。
2. 修汽车时，我弄得一_____都是机油。
3. 运动后，我一_____都是汗。
4. 今天家里大请客，只见一_____都是客人。
5. 他被车子撞到，弄得一_____都是血。

（二）Complete the sentences with "只能"。

| 开车时 | | |
|---|---|---|
| 在图书馆借书 | 只能 | |
| 下大雨时 | | |

古代农村生活，明朝沈周画，收藏于北京故宫博物院。
Painting by *Ming Dynasty* artist *Shen Zhou*, depicting farm life. *Beijing Palace Museum*

## 说文解字
## Chinese Characters

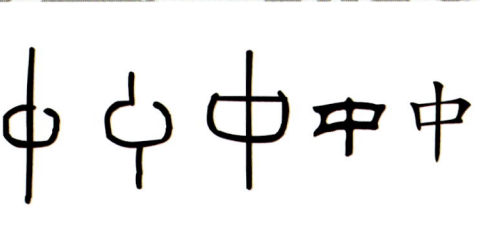

　　中国的"中"字就像旗子挂在旗杆的中间。在古代,"中"就是旗子的意思。又因为旗子挂在旗杆中间,"中"就有了"中间"的意思。古代中国人认为他们的国家在世界的中心,所以他们就叫他们的国家"中国",这种叫法一直用到了现在。

### 生字词

| | | |
|---|---|---|
| 旗子 | qí zi | flag |
| 挂 | guà | to hang |
| 旗杆 | qí gān | mast |
| 中间 | zhōng jiān | in the middle of |
| 意思 | yì si | meaning |
| 古代 | gǔ dài | ancient times |
| 认为 | rèn wéi | to think, to consider |
| 中心 | zhōng xīn | center |
| 一直 | yì zhí | all the time, always |
| 叫法 | jiào fǎ | ways to address people or things |

 妙语如珠　Words & Phrases

lóng fēi fèng wǔ
**龙飞凤舞**

"The dragon is flying while the phoenix is dancing."
This is used to describe a free and creative style of writing characters.

lóng fèng chéng xiáng
**龙凤呈祥**

"The Dragon and Phoenix bring prosperity."

　　龙和凤是中国传统的吉祥物。龙和凤在一起象征着幸运、成功、美好。中文里有很多关于龙和凤的成语，例如："龙飞凤舞"和"龙凤呈祥"。

　　龙在天上飞，凤在空中舞，非常美丽壮观。中国人常常用"龙飞凤舞"这个词来形容一个人的字写得潇洒，活泼，有创意。

　　"龙凤呈祥"是说龙和凤一起出现，象征吉祥富贵。在北京故宫里，有很多龙和凤的装饰，中国很多工艺品上也有龙和凤的图案。

### 生字词

| | | |
|---|---|---|
| 吉祥物 | jí xiáng wù | a lucky charm |
| 成功 | chéng gōng | success |
| 幸运 | xìng yùn | luck |
| 美好 | měi hǎo | fine, wonderful |
| 成语 | chéng yǔ | idiom |
| 空中 | kōng zhōng | in the sky |
| 壮观 | zhuàng guān | splendid |
| 形容 | xíng róng | to describe |
| 潇洒 | xiāo sǎ | free-spirited |
| 活泼 | huó pō | vivid, lively |
| 有创意 | yǒu chuàng yì | creative |
| 装饰 | zhuāng shì | decoration |
| 工艺品 | gōng yì pǐn | artwork, handy craft |
| 图案 | tú àn | pattern, motif |

# 华夏文化
# Chinese Culture

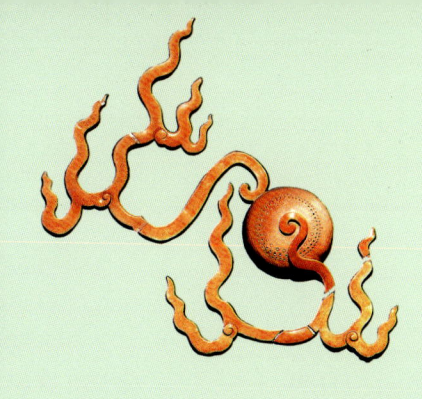

## 龙和凤

"龙"和"凤"都是中国古代神话中的动物。

"龙"强壮有力，代表着健康。它会飞翔，所以也代表着自由。这些好的意义加在一起，代表着成功。

从前，"龙"是皇帝的象征。皇帝的身体叫龙体，皇帝坐的椅子叫龙椅，皇帝的儿子叫龙子。在北京故宫里有很多龙的装饰。

龙也是中国的象征。过春节的时候，中国人喜欢舞龙；过端午节的时候，中国人喜欢赛龙舟。龙是十二生肖中的动物之一。

"凤"也叫"凤凰"，在古代是皇后的象征，它有美丽、吉祥的意思。皇后戴的王冠叫"凤冠"，后来成为中国女子结婚时喜欢戴的头饰。

"龙"和"凤"在一起，象征着成功、健康、美好、幸福。

中国父母盼望孩子长大之后会成功、幸福，因此很注意孩子的学习，人们说这是"望子成龙"。中国人为儿女起名时也常常会用"龙"、"凤"，表达对子女的美好祝愿。

九龙壁
The *Nine Dragon Wall*

## 生字词

| | | |
|---|---|---|
| 强壮有力 | qiáng zhuàng yǒu lì | strong |
| 代表 | dài biǎo | to represent, to speak for |
| 飞翔 | fēi xiáng | to fly |
| 自由 | zì yóu | freedom |
| 意义 | yì yì | meaning |
| 皇帝 | huáng dì | Emperor |
| 装饰 | zhuāng shì | decoration |
| 望子成龙 | wàng zǐ chéng lóng | to expect one's son to be talented |
| 舞龙 | wǔ lóng | Dragon Dance |
| 之一 | zhī yī | one of |
| 吉祥 | jí xiáng | lucky, auspicious |
| 皇后 | huáng hòu | Empress |
| | | |
| 戴 | dài | to wear (used for accessories like hats, belts, scarfs, watches, etc.) |
| 王冠 | wáng guàn | crown |
| 女子 | nǚ zǐ | female |
| 结婚 | jié hūn | marry |
| 头饰 | tóu shì | headwear |
| 盼望 | pàn wàng | to hope |
| 注意 | zhù yì | to pay attention to |
| 起名 | qǐ míng | to name |
| 表达 | biǎo dá | to express |
| 美好 | měi hǎo | nice, good |
| 幸福 | xìng fú | happiness |
| 祝愿 | zhù yuàn | to wish |

## The Dragon and the Phoenix

The phoenix and dragon are important symbols in Chinese culture, and are found all around the Imperial Palace and across China. The dragon has represented the Emperor and been a symbol of China in general for thousands of years. The phoenix is the sovereign of all the birds and represents the Queen. Historical sites in Beijing and around China frequently feature the dragon and phoenix. Annual events like the Dragon Boat festival revolve around them as well.

双龙玉器
A jade piece with two dragon-heads

## Dìyī jí  Wǒmen yào qù Zhōngguó

Wáng Xiǎolóng jiā —

Wáng Dàlì: Xiǎolóng, Xiǎofèng, gàosu nǐmen yí gè hǎo xiāoxi! Wǒmen yào qù Zhōngguó lǚxíng le!

Xiǎolóng: Zhēnde ma? Shénme shíhou?

Wáng Dàlì: Fùhuó jié jiàqī, jiù shì xiàgeyuè.

Xiǎofèng: Māma, wèishénme yào qù Zhōngguó? Zhōngguó hǎowán ma?

Lǐ Měilán: Dāngrán le, nǐmen kěyǐ jiàn dào yéye nǎinai, cānguān hěnduō gǔjì, chī dìdào de Zhōngguó cài, kàn kě'ài de xióngmāo, hé Zhōngguó xiǎopéngyou yìqǐ wán…Nǐmen de Zhōngwén huì jìnbù o!

Wáng Dàlì: Chúle wǒmen jiā, háiyǒu zhāng shūshu yì jiā, Joy, Ruby dōu huì qù.

Lǐ Měilán: Wǒde péngyou Smith yì jiā yě qù, nǐmen yílùshang dōu yǒu péngyou.

Xiǎolóng: Tài bàng le!


Smith Jiā —

Linda: Jason, David! Xiàgeyuè wǒmen yào qù Zhōngguó lǚxíng le!

Jason: Tài bàng le! Wǒmen shìbushì néng kàn dào chángchéng?

David: Peking Duck! Peking Duck…

Linda: Háizimen, tīngzhe: Zài Zhōngguó nǐmen zhǐnéng shuō Zhōngwén!

David: ō! Bù!

Mike: Do I have to speak Chinese?

Linda: Dāngrán.

Mike: "Nǐhǎo"、"Zàijiàn"、"Wǒ ài nǐ".

Linda: Nǐ kěyǐ mànmān xué. Nǐ zuì hǎo gěi nǐde érzimen zuò ge hǎo bǎngyàng. Kàn nǐ shìbushì zhēnde ài wǒ.


Joy Jiā —

Zhāng Huá: Nǐmen yào dài de dōngxi zhǔnbèi hǎo le ma?

Joy: Māma hé wǒ yǐjīng zhǔnbèi hǎo le, kěshì Ruby hái zài máng.

Zhāng Huá: Ruby, nǐ zài zhǎo shénme?

Ruby: Wǒ xiǎng dài wǒde bābǐ, háiyǒu wǒ xǐhuan de bǐnggān.

Zhāng Huá: Ruby, wǒmen shì qù Zhōngguó, bú shì qù lùyíng. Zài Zhōngguó yě kěyǐ mǎidào nǐ xǐhuan de bǐnggān.

Ruby: Zhōngguó yǒu màidāngláo ma?

Zhāng huá: Dāngrán yǒu! Zhōngguó háiyǒu hǎo duō nǐ xiǎngbúdào de hǎo dōngxi ne. Nǐ yídìng huì wán de hěn kāixīn de!.

# Chapter 1: We Are Going To China

WANG Dali: Xiaolong, Xiaofeng, I have good news for you. We are going to China.
Xiaolong: Really? When?
WANG Dali: During Easter, next month.
Xiaofeng: Mom, will it be fun in China?
LI Meilan: Definitely. You will see your Grandma and Grandpa, visit historical sites, try real Chinese food, see the pandas, and play with Chinese children…More importantly, you'll get to practice your Chinese.
WANG Dali: The Zhang family, Joy and Ruby, will also join us.
LI Meilan: My friend Linda and her family will come along, too.
Xiaolong: Cool.

Linda: Jason, David, we will go to China next month.
Jason: Great. We're going to climb the Great Wall.
David: Peking Duck! Peking Duck…
Linda: Boys, listen. In China, you can ONLY speak Chinese.
David: Oh, no.
Mike: Do I have to speak Chinese, too?
Linda: Absolutely. I mean "*dang ran*".
Mike: Sure, "*ni hao*," "*zai jian*," "*wo ai ni*".
Linda: You'll learn. You'd better set a good example for your sons. Let's see if you really mean "*wo ai ni*".


ZHANG Hua: Have you finished packing?
Joy: Mom and I are done. Ruby hasn't finished it yet.
ZHANG Hua: Ruby, what are you looking for?
Ruby: I want to bring my Barbie doll and my favorite cookies.
ZHANG Hua: Ruby, we are going to China, not camping.
Ruby: Is there McDonald's in China?
ZHANG Hua: Of course. China has plenty of interesting places and things you will never expect. Trust me, you will have a good time.

北京故宫的太和殿,皇帝与大臣在此议事。
The *Hall of Supreme Harmony* in the *Forbidden City* where the Emperor held audiences with ministers

# 第二集
# 集合

Chapter 2
The Group Gathers

# 第二集 集合
...... The Group Gathers

# 第二集 集合
###### The Group Gathers

## 课文 Text

# 第二集 集 合

王大力：张华、Mary，好久不见！最近怎么样？
张 华：还不错。你们呢？
李美兰：老样子。
Mary：这是小龙和小凤吧？你们好。
小龙、小凤：您好！
李美兰：Joy, Ruby 都长这么高了！
Joy, Ruby：美兰阿姨好！
王小龙：嗨！Joy, Ruby，你们好。
Joy：嗨！小龙！嗨！小凤！

王大力：你的朋友 Linda 一家怎么还没有来？
李美兰：来了！来了！在那边。嗨！Linda！
Linda：嗨！你们好！不好意思，让你们久等了！介绍一下，这是我老公 Mike，我的两个儿子 Jason 和 David。
王大力：你好！我是美兰的先生，叫我大力就好。这位是我的朋友张华，这是他太太 Mary。
Mike：你们好！我是 Mike。
张 华：你会说中文，太好了！
Linda：他能听懂中文，但是只会说"你好"、"再见"，别的就不行了。Mike，这两位就是你的中文老师了。
Mike：太好了！

王小龙：我叫王小龙，这是我的妹妹王小凤。这是 Joy，这是 Ruby.
Jason：很高兴认识你们。
David：Hi guys!
Linda：David，说中文，记住了吗？我有一个主意，我们来一个比赛，从现在开始，我们都要说中文。如果谁忘记了，就扣一分。现在每人有100分，旅行结束以后，比比谁的分数高。输的人请客，好吗？
大 家：好主意！
Mike：Wait a minute, what about me?
Linda：Mike！扣一分！
Mike：OK！我的意思是"可以！可以！"

## 生字词 Vocabulary

| | | |
|---|---|---|
| 集合 | jí hé | to gather together |
| 最近 | zuì jìn | recently |
| 不错 | bú cuò | not bad, pretty good |
| 样子 | yàng zi | appearance, look |
| 老样子 | lǎo yàng zi | (remain) the same |
| 这么 | zhè me | such, so |
| 阿姨 | ā yí | Auntie |
| 嗨 | hāi | Hi, Hello |
| 边 | biān | [suffix, signifying direction] |
| 不好意思 | bù hǎo yì si | to feel shy or embarrassed (used as an apology) |
| 让 | ràng | to let |
| 老公 | lǎo gōng | husband |
| 先生 | xiān sheng | Mr., Sir; husband |
| 太太 | tài tai | Mrs.; wife |
| 懂 | dǒng | to understand |
| 但是 | dàn shì | but |
| 别的 | bié de | other |
| 记住 | jì zhu | to remember |
| 主意 | zhǔ yi | idea |
| 开始 | kāi shǐ | to begin, to start |
| 忘记 | wàng jì | to forget |
| 扣 | kòu | to deduct |
| 结束 | jié shù | to finish |
| 分数 | fēn shù | mark, score |
| 输 | shū | to lose |
| 请客 | qǐng kè | to invite |
| 意思 | yì si | meaning |

# 语法 Grammar

## 好

① Used to mean "very" in front of descriptive adjectives.
好久，好多。

② Used as a greeting, asking how somebody is.
你好！阿姨好！

③ Good, fine, nice.
好主意！好极了！

你会说中文吗？
我会说一点儿。

## 呢、吗、吧

Particles used at the end of a sentence.

① 吗 indicates a question.
明天小龙来吗？
Is Xiaolong coming tomorrow?

② 呢 indicates a question and is often used in rhetorical questions, or to mean "what about...?"

人呢？都到哪里去了？
Where did everyone go?

③ 吧 is used to imply doubt or a suggestion.

他明天不会去北京吧？
He's not going to Beijing tomorrow, is he?

## 都

① all

我们都是大华中学的学生。
We are all students from Da Hua High School.

大家都爱学习华语。
All of us like to learn Chinese.

② already

她都已经是中学生了。
She is already a high school student.

都已经七点了。
It's already 7 o'clock.

## 如果…，就… "if…, then…"

如果明天下雨，我们就不去露营了。
If it rains tomorrow, we will not go camping.

如果你不去，就叫他去吧。
If you don't want to come, then ask him to go.

# 个、位

个 and 位 are both measure words. 个 can be used for people or things, but 位 is a polite measure word only used before people.

### ① 个

小龙都吃了两个苹果了，还要吃第三个。
Xiaolong has eaten two apples, but he still wants to eat one more.

教室里只有三个人。
There are only three people in the classroom.

### ② 位

家里来了几位客人。
A few guests are coming to my house.

这位老师是我的中文老师。
This teacher is my Chinese teacher.

长安大戏院
*The Chang-An Grand Theater*

## 练习例句 Sample exercises

（一） Use 不但...而且... to complete the sentences.

◆例句：小凤聪明，努力学习
　　　　小凤不但聪明，而且努力学习。

1. 我们的学校很大，很漂亮。
   _____

2. 他会说中文，说得非常好。
   _____

3. 她去过中国，去过好几次。
   _____

（二） What should you say in these situations?

| | |
|---|---|
| 第一次见面 | |
| 做介绍的时候 | |
| 和自己的朋友打招呼 | |
| 和爸爸妈妈的朋友打招呼 | |
| 迟到时 | |
| 拒绝别人的请求时 | |

1. 你好！最近怎么样？
2. 阿姨好！叔叔好！
3. 你好！我叫Mike，很高兴认识你。
4. 你好！这位是我的朋友Susan。
5. 对不起，我有事，不能去。
6. 对不起，我来晚了。

# 说文解字
## Chinese Characters

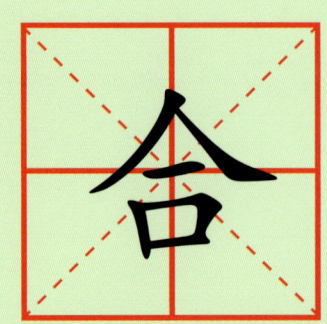

"合"的意思是聚集在一起。大家到相同的地方，叫"集合"，很多人一起唱歌叫"合唱"。"合"字很好写，它由三个字组成：人、一、口，就像每个人都有一张嘴。如果大家张嘴说一样的话，像一个人说话，就会很整齐。

### 生字词

| | | |
|---|---|---|
| 聚集 | jù jí | to assemble, to combine |
| 相同 | xiāng tóng | the same |
| 地方 | dì fang | place |
| 组成 | zǔ chéng | to form into, to gather into, to build up |
| 张 | zhāng | [a measure word for paper]; to open |
| 整齐 | zhěng qí | even and orderly, uniform |

妙语如珠　Words & Phrases

yì yán wéi dìng
### 一言为定

"One Word Makes a Decision"
This is used to mean "It is a deal."

yì xīn yí yì
### 一心一意

"One Heart One Mind"
It is used to describe someone as being determined and focused.

Linda: 马上就要去旅行了，从现在开始我们都不能说英文，只能说中文。
王大力：一言为定！
David: 什么是"一言为定"？
Linda: "一言为定"就是一句话说定了，不再改变。英文就是 It's a deal.
David: Oh, I see!
小　龙：David, 要说中文！
David: 哦！好，一言为定！
Linda: 这就对了。学中文的时候还要一心一意。
David: "一心一意"又是什么意思？一个"心"的意思？
王大力：在这里就是说你学习中文的时候很认真，不想别的事情。
David: 好，一言为定！我会一心一意地学中文。

### 生字词

| 马上 | mǎ shàng | at once, immediately |
| 定 | dìng | to decide, to agree upon |
| 改变 | gǎi biàn | to change, to alter |
| 认真 | rèn zhēn | earnest |

"合"加"口"是什么？
哈. 哈哈..

我们还可以这样说：
① A：我们明天八点在学校见。
　 B：好的，一言为定。
　 A: Let's meet at 8 at school tomorrow.
　 B: Okay, it's settled.
② A：这次比赛我们一定要得金牌！
　 B：一言为定，加油！
　 A: We must win the gold in this competition.
　 B: It's a deal, go for it!
③ 妹妹画画的时候总是一心一意的。
　 My young sister is always very focused when she is drawing.

# 华夏文化
# Chinese Culture

## 中文的称呼

中国人很讲究"礼",对不同的人有不同的称呼,如果叫错了就不礼貌。

称呼同辈的人,叫名字就可以了。长辈称呼晚辈,也可以叫名字。但是晚辈一定不能叫长辈的名字。

和熟人见面时,如果是爸爸妈妈的朋友,要叫"叔叔""伯伯"或"阿姨";如果是和爷爷年龄差不多的人,要叫"爷爷""奶奶"。称呼时,可以在前面加上姓名,如,美兰阿姨,王爷爷,张叔叔。见到不认识的老人,要叫"老人家"。坐出租车时,可以叫出租车司机"师傅"。

中国人夫妻之间的称呼也很多,丈夫可以叫对方"妻子"、"老婆"、"太太",妻子可以叫对方"丈夫"、"老公"、"先生"。

在中国人生活中,正确的称呼是对别人的尊重和礼貌,是中国文化的一个重要部分。

### 生字词

| 讲究 | jiǎng jiu | pay attention to; strive for; be particular about |
| 礼 | lǐ | etiquette, manners; gift |
| 礼貌 | lǐ mào | respect, politeness |
| 称呼 | chēng hu | addressing someone |
| 长辈 | zhǎng bèi | the older generation |
| 晚辈 | wǎn bèi | the younger generation |
| 同辈 | tóng bèi | the same generation |
| 熟人 | shú rén | acquaintance |
| 加上 | jiā shang | to add |
| 老人家 | lǎo ren jia | old folk |
| 司机 | sī jī | driver |
| 师傅 | shī fu | master |
| 之间 | zhī jiān | between |
| 丈夫 | zhàng fu | husband |
| 妻子、老婆 | qī zi, lǎo po | wife |
| 对方 | duì fāng | other side |

### Addressing people in Chinese

In Chinese there are numerous polite terms to address people, and the usage of these terms may depend on the user's age and relationship to the addressed. For example, children address their parent's friends as "Shu Shu" and "A Yi" (Uncle and Aunt) and generally refer to old people as "Ye Ye" and "Nai Nai" (Grandpa and Grandma), or "Lao Ren Jia" (old folk). Taxi drivers are frequently called "Shifu" (master). These various terms of addressing can be confusing at the beginning, but will come to be a pleasant and respectful way of interacting with people in China.

## Dìèr jí  Jíhé

Wáng Dàlì: Zhāng Huá, Mary, hǎo jiǔ bú jiàn! Zuìjìn zěnmeyàng?
Zhāng Huá: Hái búcuò.  Nǐmen ne?
Lǐ Měilán: Lǎo yàngzi.
Mary: Zhè shì Xiǎolóng hé Xiǎofèng ba? Nǐmen hǎo.
Xiǎolóng, Xiǎofèng: Nín hǎo!
Lǐ Měilán: Joy, Ruby dōu zhǎng zhème gāo le!
Joy, Ruby: Měilán āyí hǎo!
Xiǎolóng: Hāi! Joy, Ruby, nǐmen hǎo.
Joy: Hāi! Xiǎolóng! Hāi! Xiǎofèng!

Wáng Dàlì: Nǐ de péngyou Linda yìjiā zěnme hái méiyou lái?
Lǐ Měilán: Lái le! Lái le! Zài nà biān.  Hāi! Linda!
Linda: Hāi! Nǐmen hǎo! Bùhǎoyìsi, ràng nǐmen jiǔ děng le! Jièshào yí xià, zhè shì wǒ lǎogōng Mike, wǒde liǎng gè érzi Jason hé David.
Wáng Dàlì: Nǐhǎo! Wǒ shì měilán de xiānsheng, jiào wǒ Dàlì jiù hǎo.  Zhè wèi shì wǒde péngyou zhāng Huá, zhè shì tā tàitai Mary.
Mike: Nǐmen hǎo! Wǒ shì Mike.
Zhāng Huá: Nǐ huì shuō Zhōngwén, tàihǎole!
Linda: Tā néng tīng dǒng Zhōngwén, dànshì zhǐ huì shuō "nǐhǎo", "zàijiàn", biéde jiù bù xíng le.  Mike, zhè liǎng wèi jiù shì nǐ de Zhōngwén lǎoshī le.
Mike: Tàihǎole!

Xiǎolóng: Wǒ jiào Wáng Xiǎolóng, zhè shì wǒde mèimei Wáng Xiǎofèng.  Zhè shì Joy, zhè shì Ruby.
Jason: Hěn gāoxìng rènshi nǐmen.
David: Hi guys!
Linda: David, shuō Zhōngwén, jìzhu le ma? Wǒ yǒu yí gè zhǔyi, wǒmen lái yí gè bǐsài, cóng xiànzài kāishǐ, wǒmen dōu yào shuō Zhōngwén.  Rúguǒ shuí wàngjì le, jiù kòu yì fēn.  Xiànzài měirén yǒu yìbǎi fēn, lǚxíng jiéshù yǐhòu, bǐ bǐ shuí de fēnshù gāo.  Shū de rén qǐngkè, hǎo ma?
Dà jiā: Hǎo zhǔyi!
Mike: Wait a minute, what about me?
Linda: Mike! Kòu yì fēn!
Mike: OK! Wǒde yìsi shì "Kěyǐ! Kěyǐ!"

# Chapter 2: The Group Gathers

WANG Dali: ZHANG Hua, Mary, how's it going?
ZHANG Hua: Not bad.  How about you?
LI Meilan: Same as usual.
Mary: You must be Xiaolong and Xiaofeng.  Nice to meet you.
Xiaolong, Xiaofeng:  Nice to meet you.
LI Meilan: Joy, Ruby, what big girls you are now!
Joy, Ruby: Hello Auntie Meilan.
Xiaolong: Hey Joy.  Hey Ruby.
Joy: Hi Xiaolong.  Hi Xiaofeng.

WANG Dali: Where's your friend Linda and her family?
LI Meilan: They're over there.  Hi Linda.
Linda: Hello everyone. Sorry to keep you waiting.  This is my husband, Mike, and my sons, Jason and David.
WANG Dali: Hello. I'm Meilan's husband--just call me Dali.  This is my friend ZHANG Hua and his wife Mary.
Mike: *Ni men hao.  Wo jiao* Mike.
ZHANG Hua: You can speak Chinese?  That's wonderful.
Linda: He can understand what we say, but he doesn't speak much Chinese except *ni hao* and *zai jian*.  Mike, they are your Chinese teachers.
Mike: Great.

Xiaolong: My name is Xiaolong. This is my sister Xiaofeng.  This is Joy and this is Ruby.
Jason: Nice to meet you.
David: Hi guys.
Linda: David, remember--speak Chinese. I have an idea.  Let's have a competition.  Everybody must speak Chinese from now on.  Each time you forget, you lose one point.  Everybody starts with 100 points.  At the end of the trip, let's compare scores and the loser has to treat everyone, how's that?
Others: OK. Good idea.
Mike: Wait a minute, what about me?
Linda: Mike, you lose one point.
Mike: OK. I mean— *"keyi, keyi"*.

# 第三集
# Cola 就是可乐

### Chapter 3
### Cola is *Kele*

# 第三集　Cola 就是可乐
······ Cola is *Kele*

# 第三集　Cola 就是可乐
…… Cola is *Kele*

## 课文 Text

### 第三集　Cola 就是可乐

空中服务员：飞机马上就要起飞了，请大家系好安全带。

服务员：您好！请问，您想喝什么饮料？
Linda: 咖啡。
服务员：要加牛奶吗？
Linda: 不用，糖就可以了，谢谢。你们想喝什么？
Jason: 我要橙汁。
David: Cola.
Jason: 妈妈，David没有说中文！扣一分！
Linda: 没有呀，我听见David说的是中文。他不是要可乐吗？

Jason: 可乐？Cola？
David: 哈哈！Cola就是可乐。Chinese, English, what's the difference?!
Linda & Jason (齐说)：扣一分！

服务员：请填写入境卡。
王大力：谢谢。小龙，小凤，这是你们的入境卡。
小　龙：我的 passport number 是什么？
王大力：702016788。

小　龙："Passport" 中文怎么说？
王大力：护照。
小　凤：目的地是哪里？
王大力：北京。
小　凤：北京现在几点了？
王大力：我看看，应该是下午三点多，北京比加州早15个小时。
小　龙：还有多久才到北京呀？我已经去了三次洗手间了。
王大力：差不多还有两个小时。我们的奇妙中国游就要开始喽！

 生字词 Vocabulary

| | | |
|---|---|---|
| 空中服务员 | kōng zhōng fú wù yuán | flight attendant |
| 马上 | mǎ shàng | right away |
| 起飞 | qǐ fēi | to take off |
| 系 | jì | to tie, to buckle |
| 安全带 | ān quán dài | seat belt |
| 加 | jiā | to add |
| 橙汁 | chéng zhī | orange juice |
| 呀 | ya | [particle signifying emphasis] |
| 听见 | tīng jiàn | to hear, heard |
| 哈 | hā | ha [laughter] |
| 填写 | tián xiě | to fill in |
| 入境卡 | rù jìng kǎ | entry card |
| 护照 | hù zhào | passport |
| 目的地 | mù dì dì | destination |
| 加州 | jiā zhōu | California |
| 早 | zǎo | early |
| 小时 | xiǎo shí | hour |
| 才 | cái | [an adverb indicating that something has taken place later than usual or expected] |
| 次 | cì | time |
| 洗手间 | xǐ shǒu jiān | washroom |
| 差不多 | chà bu duō | approximately, about |
| 奇妙 | qí miào | magical, wonderful |
| 游 | yóu | tour, journey |
| 喽 | lou | [particle indicating the sentence is a statement] |

你想做空中服务员吗?

想, 因为可以飞来飞去。

 语法 Grammar

## 就要, 马上就要

It means "about to", "will soon".

我们马上就要到北京了。
We will arrive in Beijing soon.

你再等会儿好吗？小龙马上就要回来了。
Could you wait a minute? Xiaolong will be back in a minute.

## 不是…吗？／…不是吗？

This is a rhetorical question. "不是…吗？" can also be changed into "…不是吗？", which means "… right?", "Doesn't… ?" or "Isn't it… ?".

小龙不是会说中文吗？
Doesn't Xiaolong speak Chinese?

小龙会说中文，不是吗？
Xiaolong can speak Chinese, can't he?

## 看看

When a verb is doubled, it means the action is casual, like the English "… a bit" or "… a little".

你听听，那边有人在唱歌。
Listen, someone is singing over there.

我想到游乐场去玩玩。
I want to play for a bit in the amusement park.

## 才

"才" indicates something late in coming. "还有多久" means "how much longer?".

我想家了，还有多久才回家呀？
I miss my home. How much longer before we go home?

都两个小时了。还有多久才到北京呀？
It's already been two hours. How many more hours before we arrive in Beijing?

## 了…了

The first "了" is an active auxiliary word, which indicates that the act has been completed. The second "了" indicates the sentence is a statement.

我已经吃了两个苹果了。
I have eaten two apples already.

小凤已经写了五篇日记了。
Xiaofeng has already written five diary entries.

## 练习例句　Sample exercises

（一）Rewrite the following sentences with 不是...吗？/ 不是吗？

◆ 例句：她喜欢唱中国歌。

　　她 不是 喜欢唱中国歌 吗？

　　她喜欢唱中国歌，不是吗？

1. 小凤不会说中文。

　　_____不是_____吗？

　　_____不是吗？

2. David 总被扣分。

　　_____不是 _____吗？

　　_____不是吗？

3. 王大力要去美国旅游。

　　_____不是_____吗？

　　_____不是吗？

（二）What would they say or do in these situations?

| | |
|---|---|
| 飞机要起飞时，空中服务员说 | 请大家系好安全带 |
| 空中服务员问乘客 | |
| Jason 的妈妈说：我们都要说中文，说英语要 | |
| 下飞机前，空中服务员提醒乘客 | |
| 去外国旅游要 | |

## 说文解字
## Chinese Characters

古装美女木偶
Wood carving of a traditional Chinese beauty

"妙"字有两个部分:"女"和"少"。"女"是female的意思,"少"可以读shào,是"年轻"的意思。少女,就是年轻的女孩,给人很美好的感觉。"妙"就是美好的意思。和"妙"有关的词语有"美妙"、"奇妙"、"妙语"等等。

### 生字词

| | | |
|---|---|---|
| 部分 | bù fen | part, section |
| 年轻 | nián qīng | young |
| 美好 | měi hǎo | nice, wonderful |
| 感觉 | gǎn jué | feeling |
| 有关 | yǒu guān | relevant |
| 美妙 | měi miào | wonderful |
| 妙语 | miào yǔ | fun words |

## 妙语如珠 Words & Phrases

**bǎi wén bù rú yí jiàn**
**百闻不如一见**

"Hearing 100 times is not as good as seeing once."
This idiom is used to demonstrate the value of seeing something once for yourself over hearing about it again and again from others. "A picture is worth a thousand words" and "seeing is believing" are English phrases that are used in similar situations.

**qiān lǐ zhī xíng, shǐ yú zú xià**
**千里之行,始于足下**

"A journey of a thousand Li begins under one's feet."
This is used to mean that great tasks are accomplished one step at a time.

要去中国旅游了,Jason 和 David 都很兴奋。这是他们第一次去中国旅游,有很多想知道的东西。Jason 问妈妈:"长城和电影里一样吗?我听说长城有一万里长,是真的吗?"David 也问:"北京烤鸭好吃吗?我们还能吃到什么中国菜?"他们的问题太多了,Linda 一下子没法回答,她想了想,说:"百闻不如一见,到了中国你们就知道了!"Jason 说:"我等不及了。真想现在就飞到中国去!"Linda 笑着说:"中国人常说'千里之行,始于足下',意思就是去非常远的地方也要从脚下的第一步开始。旅行的第一步就是整理好要带的东西。你们整理好了吗?"David 和 Jason 一起说:"现在就去整理!"

### 生字词

| | | |
|---|---|---|
| 闻 | wén | to hear, heard |
| 兴奋 | xīng fèn | excited |
| 问题 | wèn tí | question, problem |
| 回答 | huí dá | to answer |
| 里 | lǐ | Chinese mile (half a kilometer) |
| 应该 | yīng gāi | should, ought to |
| 第一步 | dì yī bù | the first step |

我们还可以这样说:
① 见到长城之后才发现真的太棒了,真是百闻不如一见。
The great wall is so great that after visiting it, people say hearing about it 100 times is not as good as seeing it once.
② 千里之行始于足下,要想有好的身体,要坚持每天锻炼才可以。
A thousand Li journey starts under your feet. You should exercise everyday if you want to be healthy.

## 华夏文化
## Chinese Culture

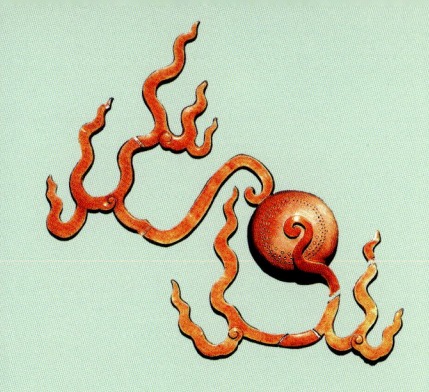

### 北京在哪里？

奇妙中国游开始了，你知道我们的目的地——北京在哪里吗？北京在中国北方的河北省，是中国的首都。北京是个有三千多年历史的大都市，它在公元1260年成为元朝的首都——元大都。在明朝时改名为北京，成为明朝的首都，在之后的七百多年里几乎都是中国的首都。北京有很多有名的古迹：长城、故宫、颐和园、天坛等等。北京现在是个又古老又现代的大都市。2008年的奥运会在这座城市举行。

### 生字词

| | | |
|---|---|---|
| 省 | shěng | province |
| 首都 | shǒu dū | capital |
| 大都市 | dà dū shì | metropolis |
| 公元 | gōng yuán | A.D. |
| 改名 | gǎi míng | to rename |
| 颐和园 | yí hé yuán | the Summer Palace |
| 天坛 | tiān tán | the Temple of Heaven |
| 古老 | gǔ lǎo | ancient |
| 现代 | xiàn dài | modern |
| 奥运会 | ào yùn huì | Olympic Games |
| 举行 | jǔ xíng | to hold; to be held |

### Where is Beijing?

Beijing, which means "North Capital", is the capital of China and a city of nearly 15 million people. Home to the Emperor and also known as the Imperial City, Beijing is the location of such important historical sites as the Forbidden City, the Great Wall, the Summer Palace and the Temple of Heaven. Beijing rose to prominence relatively late in Chinese history and its major monuments were built between 200 and 500 years ago.

奇妙中国游 — MAGICAL TOUR OF CHINA

# Dìsān jí  Cola jiùshì kělè

Kōngzhōngfúwùyuán: Fēijī mǎshàng jiù yào qǐfēi le, qǐng dàjiā jì hǎo ānquándài.

Fúwùyuán: Nínhǎo! Qǐngwèn, nín xiǎng hē shénme yǐnliào?
Linda: Kāfēi.
Kōngjiě: Yào jiā niúnǎi ma?
Linda: Bú yòng, táng jiù kěyǐ le, xièxie. Nǐmen xiǎng hē shénme?
Jason: Wǒ yào chéngzhī.
David: Cola.
Jason: Māma, David méiyǒu shuō Zhōngwén! Kòu yì fēn!
Linda: Méiyǒu ya, wǒ tīngjiàn David shuō de shì Zhōngwén. Tā búshì yào kělè ma?
Jason: Kělè? Cola?
David: Hāha, Cola jiù shì kělè. Chinese, English, what's the difference?!
Linda & Jason (qíshuō): Kòu yì fēn!

Fúwùyuán: Qǐng tiánxiě rùjìngkǎ.
Wáng Dàlì: Xièxie. Xiǎolóng, Xiǎofèng, zhè shì nǐmen de rùjìngkǎ.
Xiǎolóng: Wǒ de passport number shì shénme?
Wáng Dàlì: 702016788.
Xiǎolóng: "Passport" Zhōngwén zěnme shuō?
Wáng Dàlì: Hùzhào.
Xiǎofèng: Mùdìdì shì nǎli?
Wáng Dàlì: Běijīng.
Xiǎofèng: Běijīng xiànzài jǐ diǎn le?
Wáng Dàlì: Wǒ kàn kan, yīnggāi shì xiàwǔ sān diǎn duō, Běijīng bǐ jiāzhōu zǎo 15 ge xiǎoshí.
Xiǎolóng: Háiyǒu duō jiǔ cái dào Běijīng ya? Wǒ yǐjīng qù le sāncì xǐshǒujiān le.
Wáng Dàlì: Chàbuduō háiyǒu liǎng ge xiǎoshí. Wǒmen de qímiào Zhōngguó yóu jiù yào kāishǐ lou!

# Chapter 3: Cola is *Kele*

Flight attendant: The plane is going to take off. Please fasten your seat belts.

Flight attendant: Would you like something to drink?
Linda: Coffee, please.
Flight attendant: Milk?
Linda: No, just sugar, thank you. What would you like?
Jason: I'd like some orange juice.
David: Cola please.
Jason: Mom, David didn't speak Chinese. Take off one point.
Linda: But I heard him speaking Chinese. Didn't he say *kele*?
Jason: Cola? *Kele*?
David: Haha, cola is *kele*! Chinese, English, what's the difference?
Linda & Jason (together): Take off one point.


Flight attendant: Please fill in your entry cards.
WANG Dali: Thank you. Xiaolong, Xiaofeng, here are your entry cards.
Xiaolong: What's my passport number?
WANG Dali: 702016788.
Xiaolong: What's "passport" in Chinese?
WANG Dali: *Huzhao*.
Xiaofeng: What do I write for the destination?
WANG Dali: Beijing.
Xiaofeng: What time is it in Beijing now?
WANG Dali: Let me see…It's about 3 in the afternoon. Beijing is 15 hours ahead of California.
Xiaolong: How many more hours before we land? I've been to the bathroom three times already.
WANG Dali: About 6 more hours. Our magical tour of China is about to begin.

# 边防检查 入境登记卡

- 姓名
- 证件号码
- 签注号码
- 签注签发地
- 船名/车次/航班号
- 来自何地
- 国内住址

以上申明真实完整。如有不实填报，愿承担由此引起的一切法律责任。

签名

公安出入境管理局监制  证件种类  签证种类

## ENTRY CARD — FOR FOREIGN TRAVELLERS

PLEASE COMPLETE IN ENGLISH. FILL IN ☐ WITH ✓

- Family Name
- Given Names
- Passport No.
- Visa No.
- Place of Visa Issuance
- Flight No. Ship Name Train No.
- From
- Intended Address in China

I declare the information I have given is true, correct and complete. I understand incorrect or untrue answer to any questions may have serious con...

SIGNATURE

- Date of Birth — YEAR MONTH DAY
- Male ☐  Female ☐
- Nationality
- Your Main Reason for Coming to China (one only)
  - Convention / Conference
  - Business
  - Employment
  - Settle down
  - Visiting friends or relatives
  - Outing / in leisure
  - Study
  - Return home
  - Others

Date of Entry — YEAR MONTH DAY

OFFICIAL USE ONLY

## CHINA CUSTOMS
### BAGGAGE DECLARATION FORM FOR INCOMING PASSENGERS

Please read the instructions on the reverse side and provide information or mark "✓" in the space

1. Surname
   Given Name
2. Date of Birth — Year Month Day
3. Sex — Male ☐ Female ☐
4. No. of Traveler's Document
5. Nationality (Region) — China ( Hong Kong ☐ Macao ☐ Taiwan ☐ )  Other Nationals
6. Purpose of the Trip — Official ☐ Business ☐ Leisure ☐ Stu... Immigration ☐ Visiting Friends or Relatives ☐ Return Residents ☐ Oth...
7. Flight No./Vehicle No./ Vessel Name
8. Number of persons under the age of 16 traveling with you

I am (We are) bringing into China's Customs territory (having)

9. (residents) articles valued at over RMB 5,000 from overseas. — Yes ☐ No ☐
10. (non-residents) articles valued at over RMB 2,000 that will remain in the territory. — Yes ☐ No ☐
11. over 1,500ml (12% volume) alcoholic drinks, over 400 sticks of cigarettes, over 100 sticks of cigars, or over 500g of tobacco. — Yes ☐
12. Chinese currency in cash exceeding RMB 20,000 or foreign currencies in cash exceeding USD 5,000 if converted into US dollar. — Yes ☐
13. animals and plants, animal and plant products, microbes, biological products, human tissues, blood and blood products. — Yes ☐
14. radio transmitters, radio receivers, communication security equipments. — Yes ☐
15. other articles which are prohibited or restricted from being brought into the territory in accordance with the law of the People's Republic of China. — Yes ☐
16. unaccompanied baggage. — Yes ☐
17. goods of commercial value, samples, advertisements. — Yes ☐

I HAVE READ THE INSTRUCTIONS ON THE REVERSE SIDE OF THIS FORM AND DECLARE THAT THE INFORMATION GIVEN ON THIS FORM IS TRUE.

Passengers who are bringing any articles included in items 9-15 shall fill out this form in det...

| Description | Quantity | Value | Type/Model | Customs Rema... |
|---|---|---|---|---|
|  |  |  |  |  |
|  |  |  |  |  |
|  |  |  |  |  |
|  |  |  |  |  |

PASSENGER'S SIGNATURE     Year  Month  Date

## 中华人民共和国海关
### 进境旅客行李物品申报单

请先阅读背面的填表须知，然后在空格内填写文字信息或划 ✓

1. 姓名 — 拼音 / 中文正楷
2. 出生日期 — 年 月 日
3. 性别 — 男 ☐ 女 ☐
4. 进出境证件号码
5. 国籍（地区）— 中国（香港 ☐ 澳门 ☐ 台湾 ☐）外国
6. 进境事由 — 公务 ☐ 商务 ☐ 旅游 ☐ 学习 ☐  定居 ☐ 探亲访友 ☐ 返回居住地 ☐ 其他 ☐
7. 航班号/车次/船名
8. 同行未满16周岁人数

我（我们）携带（有）：

9. （居民旅客）在境外获取的总值超过人民币5,000元的物品 — 是 ☐ 否 ☐
10. （非居民旅客）拟留在中国境内的总值超过人民币2,000元的物品 — 是 ☐ 否 ☐
11. 超过1,500毫升酒精饮料（酒精含量12度以上），或超过400支香烟，或超过100支雪茄，或超过500克烟丝 — 是 ☐ 否 ☐
12. 超过20,000元人民币现钞，或超过折合5,000美元外币现钞 — 是 ☐ 否 ☐
13. 动植物及其产品、微生物、生物制品、人体组织、血液及其制品 — 是 ☐ 否 ☐
14. 无线电收发信机、通信保密机 — 是 ☐ 否 ☐
15. 中华人民共和国禁止和其它限制进境的物品 — 是 ☐ 否 ☐
16. 分离运输行李 — 是 ☐ 否 ☐
17. 货物、货样、广告品 — 是 ☐ 否 ☐

我已阅知本申报单背面所列事项，并保证所有申报属实。

携带有9-15项下物品的，请详细填写如下清单：

| 品名/币种 | 数量 | 金额 | 型号 | 海关批注 |
|---|---|---|---|---|
|  |  |  |  |  |
|  |  |  |  |  |
|  |  |  |  |  |
|  |  |  |  |  |

旅客签名         年 月 日

# 第四集
## 北京的车真多

Chapter 4
Beijing Has So Many Cars

# 第四集　北京的车真多
…… Beijing Has So Many Cars

# 第四集　北京的车真多
…… Beijing Has So Many Cars

## 课文 Text

# 第四集 北京的车真多

下了飞机后，王小龙和王小凤跟着爸爸妈妈上了出租车。

司　机：您好！请问您去哪儿？
王大力：您好！我们去"鼓楼大街"。
小　龙：爸爸，你以前住在"鼓楼大街"吗？
王大力：对！去美国之前我一直和你们爷爷奶奶住在那里！
小　凤：我们要住在爷爷奶奶家吗？
王大力：没错。
小　凤：那Linda阿姨和张叔叔他们住在哪里？
王大力：他们住在长城饭店。明天我们去饭店找他们。

小　龙：北京的汽车真多！
小　凤：还有那么多自行车。
王大力：你知道这些车的中文怎么说吗？
小　龙：我知道我们坐的叫"出租车"，bike是"自行车"。别的，就不知道了。
王大力：Truck是"卡车"；Bus的中文就是"巴士"，也可以叫"公共汽车"。
小　龙：哦，我懂了，中文里所有的vehicles都用"车"字。
王大力：没错！你们知道吗？中文里"坐出租车"又叫"打车"。
小　龙："打"？太好笑了！为什么要去"打一辆车"？
王大力：哈哈哈...其实不是你想的那样。"打"在中文里有很多意思，你们看：打电话、打字、打鸡蛋、打人...都用"打"字。
小　龙：打车！我一下子就记住了。

小　凤：爸爸，怎么还没到呀？
王大力：嗯...快了！看，到了！这就是爸爸的家！
司　机：车费是87块。
王大力：给您90。
司　机：找您3块。拿好您的行李，别落下东西。
王大力：谢谢。我们终于到家啦！

我们也到北京了！

## 生字词 Vocabulary

| | | |
|---|---|---|
| 车 | chē | vehicle |
| 跟 | gēn | with, to follow |
| 司机 | sī jī | driver |
| 哪儿 | nǎr | where |
| 鼓楼 | gǔ lóu | [a place in Beijing] |
| 大街 | dà jiē | street, avenue |
| 以前 | yǐ qián | before |
| 之前 | zhī qián | before |
| 没 | méi | without, no |
| 错 | cuò | mistake, wrong |
| 没错 | méi cuò | right, correct |
| 饭店 | fàn diàn | hotel |
| 那么 | nà me | so |
| 卡车 | kǎ chē | truck |
| 巴士 | bā shì | bus |
| 公共汽车 | gōng gòng qì chē | bus |
| 所有 | suǒ yǒu | all |
| 打车 | dǎ chē | to take a taxi |
| 好笑 | hǎo xiào | funny |
| 辆 | liàng | [a measure word for vehicles] |
| 其实 | qí shí | in fact, actually |
| 那样 | nà yàng | like that, that kind |
| 打字 | dǎ zì | to type |
| 打鸡蛋 | dǎ jī dàn | to take the shell off an egg |
| 打人 | dǎ rén | to beat someone |
| 一下子 | yí xià zi | at once |
| 嗯 | ng | uhm |
| 车费 | chē fèi | (taxi) fee |
| 拿 | ná | to take |
| 行李 | xíng li | luggage |
| 别 | bié | do not |
| 落 | là | left behind, to leave behind |
| 终于 | zhōng yú | at last, finally |
| 啦 | la | [ending word signifying emphasis] |

# 语法 Grammar

## 儿

"儿" is a suffix. In Mandarin Chinese, people like to add the suffix "儿" at the end of a word or a character. It is a style of informal speech.

我要去买花儿。
I want to buy some flowers.

请等一会儿。
Please wait for a while.

## 一直

Subject + 一直 + Verb
This sentence pattern means to keep on doing something without stopping.

他一直在中文学校学习中文。
He studied Chinese in a Chinese school the whole time.

雨一直下了两天两夜。
It has been raining continuously for two days and two nights.

## 打

① 用在球类运动：to play ball　打球
② 用…方法：by means of　打车
③ 殴打：to fight, to beat　打人
④ 打破：to break　打鸡蛋

## 好

We've already seen "好" being used to mean ① good, ② a greeting and ③ quite a few. Here it is used after a verb to indicate an action is finished satisfactorily.

穿好衣服，不要感冒了。
Put on all your clothes because you don't want to catch cold.

坐好了，我们要上课了。
Take your seats, the class is going to begin.

## 落

Some characters have two or more pronunciations and different meanings, they are called polyphone characters. "落" is a polyphone character with that can mean to fall or to leave something behind.

① 落 (luò) to fall, to descend

落叶 luò yè: falling leaf
降落 jiàng luò: to descend

② 落 (là) to forget something, to have left something behind

他常常把本子落在教室里面。
He always left his notebook in the classroom.

我又把书落在家里了，还得回去拿。
I left my book at home again, so I have to go back to fetch it.

## 练习例句 Sample exercises

（一）Use the correct phrase to complete the following sentences:

    一直    一天

◆ 例句：他最近三年<u>一直</u>在学中文。

1. 昨天_____，小明都不在家里。

2. 这段时间，他_____在学习汉语。

3. 小美看书看得很快，这些书她看了_____就看完了。

4. 现在是雨季，大雨_____下个不停。

（二）What should you pay attention to in these situations?

| | |
|---|---|
| 下车时 | 要注意不要把东西落在车上 |
| 游泳以前 | |
| 吃饭以前 | |
| 出去爬山 | |
| 考试以前 | |

地铁站牌
Subway sign

# 说文解字
## Chinese Characters

中国人造汉字的主要方法有四种。

最简单的方法是象形，这样造出来的字叫象形字 (ideograph, pictograph)，如：日、月、山、水。这些字的写法和他们的形状很像。

还有一种造字法是形声，造出来的字就是形声字 (phonogram)。这样的字由两部分组成，一边是字的意思，一边是字的读音。有80%的汉字是形声字。

"跟"（gēn）就是一个形声字：左边的"足"说明它的意思和脚有关；右边的"艮"（gěn）是它的读音，只有声调是不同的。所以"跟"原来的意思就是脚的后面，或是鞋的后面，现在有to follow的意思。

"根"（gēn）和"跟"一样，也是形声字。说明它的意思是"木"，和植物有关，是root的意思。

想一想你学过的字，哪些是形声字？

### 生字词

| | | |
|---|---|---|
| 造 | zào | to create |
| 主要 | zhǔ yào | main, chief |
| 简单 | jiǎn dān | easy |
| 象形字 | xiàng xíng zì | ideograph |
| 形状 | xíng zhuàng | shape |
| 说明 | shuō míng | to explain |

| | | |
|---|---|---|
| 或 | huò | or |
| 这样 | zhè yàng | in this way |
| 形声字 | xíng shēng zì | phonogram |
| 读音 | dú yīn | pronunciation |
| 声调 | shēng diào | tone |
| 植物 | zhí wù | plant |

## 妙语如珠 Words & Phrases

**wǔ huā bā mén**
**五花八门**

"5 flowers and 8 frames."
Used to describe something with great variety.

**chuān liú bù xī**
**川流不息**

"The river flows without stopping."
This describes something that goes on and on, like an endless stream.

　　北京城有那么多的城门，一下子还真记不住。中文里有一个成语很有趣，叫"五花八门"，是不是和北京的城门有关系呢？其实"五花八门"可不是五朵花和八个门的意思，它的意思是说花样很多，种类很多。在中国有很多和数字有关的成语，他们常常不是数字本来的意思。像百闻不如一见，里面的"百"是说很多，"一"的意思是很少。

　　北京的车也很多，有汽车、卡车、自行车还有公共汽车，真是五花八门。那么多的车在马路上来来往往，就可以说：北京的车真多，来来往往，川流不息。

　　"川"就是河，"流"是to flow的意思，"息"是停止的意思。"川流不息"就是河水一直流动不停止。我们可以用这个词来说人或者车很多，来来往往不停止。

### 生字词

| | | |
|---|---|---|
| 其实 | qí shí | in fact |
| 花样 | huā yàng | pattern |
| 种类 | zhǒng lèi | variety, kind |
| 来来往往 | lái lái wǎng wǎng | back and forth, come and go |
| 停止 | tíng zhǐ | to stop |

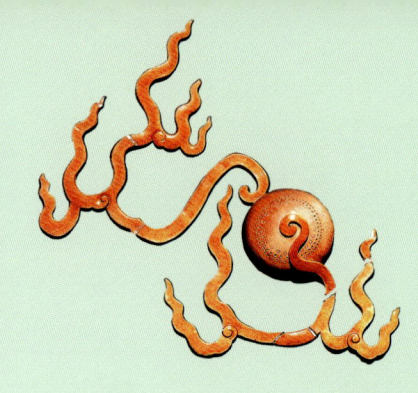

## 华夏文化
## Chinese Culture

## 北京城

　　老北京城是一座长方形的城市，故宫是城市的中心，位于长安街，与天安门广场隔街对望。长安街又被称为"中华第一街"，街道的两旁有很多古老的建筑，像故宫，也有很多新式的建筑，像东方广场。

　　老北京分为内城和外城，内城的东、西、南、北一共有九个城门。

　　北京的古迹和传统建筑大多集中在内城。北京最大的湖——前海、后海也在这里。内城还有著名的王府井商业街，被称为"东方的香榭丽舍"。内城南面有很多百年老店、茶馆和戏院。想了解老北京的风土人情，一定要去这些地方看看。

　　这些年的北京比以前扩大了许多，以故宫为中心，修建了二环路、三环路、四环路和五环路，它们像一个个圈环绕着故宫，把北京城贯通起来。外城的西北地区是大学区和科技区，著名的北京大学和中关村都在那里。东边是北京的中央商务区，处处是高楼大厦，非常繁华。

　　所以说，北京是个又古老又现代的大都市。

## 生字词

| | | |
|---|---|---|
| 长方形 | cháng fāng xíng | rectangle |
| 中心 | zhōng xīn | center |
| 城门 | chéng mén | gate |
| 内城 | nèi chéng | inner city |
| 外城 | wài chéng | outer city |
| 传统 | chuán tǒng | traditional |
| 建筑 | jiàn zhù | architecture, building |
| 大多 | dà duō | mostly, mainly |
| 湖 | hú | lake |
| 前海 | qián hǎi | Qianhai |
| 后海 | hòu hǎi | Houhai |
| 被称为 | bèi chēng wéi | be called |
| 东方的香榭丽舍 | dōng fāng de xiāng xiè lì shè | The Champs-Elysees of the East |
| 茶馆 | chá guǎn | tea house |
| 戏院 | xì yuàn | opera theater |
| 了解 | liǎo jiě | to get to know |
| 风土人情 | fēng tǔ rén qíng | local conditions and customs |
| 修建 | xiū jiàn | to build |
| 环路 | huán lù | ring road |
| 圈 | quān | ring, circle |
| 环绕 | huán rào | to circle |
| 贯通 | guàn tōng | to connect, to link up |
| 科技 | kē jì | technology |
| 高楼大厦 | gāo lóu dà shà | high buildings and large mansions |
| 繁华 | fán huá | prosperous |

## Beijing City

The ancient walled city of Beijing remained intact until mid 20th Century. Today's Beijing is basically made up of a series of concentric rectangles. At the center of the city is Tian'anmen Square and the Forbidden City, as the city expands there are five ring roads that circle all the way around. Most roads run either North/South or East/West and navigation around the city is simple.

圆形玉鱼
A fish motif in jade

# Dìsì jí  Běijīng de chēzhēn duō

Xià le fēijī hòu, Wáng Xiǎolóng hé Wáng Xiǎofèng gēn zhe bàba māma shàng le chūzūchē.

Sījī: Nín hǎo! Qǐngwèn nín qù nǎr?
Wáng Dàlì: Nín hǎo! Wǒmen qù "Gǔlóu Dàjiē".
Xiǎolóng: Bàba, nǐ yǐqián zhù zài "Gǔlóu Dàjiē" ma?
Wáng Dàlì: Duì! Qù Měiguó zhīqián wǒ yìzhí hé nǐmen yéye nǎinai zhù zài nàli!
Xiǎofèng: Wǒmen yào zhù zài yéye nǎinai jiā ma?
Wáng Dàlì: Méi cuò.
Xiǎofèng: Nà Linda āyí hé zhāng shūshu tā men zhù zài nǎli?
Wáng Dàlì: Tā men zhù zài chángchéng fàndiàn. Míngtiān wǒmen qù fàndiàn zhǎo tā men.

Xiǎolóng: Běijīng de qìchē zhēn duō!
Xiǎofèng: Háiyǒu nàme duō zìxíngchē.
Wáng Dàlì: Nǐ zhīdào zhèxiē chē de Zhōngwén zěnme shuō ma?
Xiǎolóng: Wǒ zhīdào wǒmen zuò de jiào "chūzūchē", bike shì "zìxíngchē", biéde, jiù bù zhīdao le.
Wáng Dàlì: Truck shì "kǎchē"; Bus de Zhōngwén jiù shì "bāshì", yě kěyǐ jiào "gōnggòngqìchē".
Xiǎolóng: Ò, wǒ dǒng le, Zhōngwén lǐ suǒyǒu de vehicles dōu yòng "chē" zì.
Wáng Dàlì: Méicuò! Nǐmen zhīdào ma? Zhōngwén lǐ "zuò chūzūchē" yòu jiào "dǎchē".
Xiǎolóng: "Dǎ"? Tài hǎoxiào le! Wèishénme yào qù "dǎ yí liàng chē"?
Wáng Dàlì: Hā hā hā… qíshí bú shì nǐ xiǎng de nàyàng. "Dǎ" zài Zhōngwén lǐ yǒu hěnduō yìsi, nǐmen kàn: dǎdiànhuà, dǎzì, dǎjīdàn, dǎrén… dōu yòng "dǎ" zì.
Xiǎolóng: Dǎchē! Wǒ yíxiàzi jiù jìzhù le.

Xiǎofèng: Bàba, zěnme hái méi dào ya?
Wáng Dàlì: ng… kuài le! Kàn, dào le! Zhè jiù shì bàba de jiā!
Sījī: Chēfèi shì 87 kuài.
Wáng Dàlì: Gěi nín 90.
Sījī: Zhǎo nín 3 kuài. Ná hǎo nín de xíngli, bié là xià dōngxi.
Wáng Dàlì: Xièxie. Wǒmen zhōngyú dào jiā la!

# Chapter 4: Beijing Has So Many Cars

When they get off the plane, Xiaolong and Xiaofeng get in a taxi with their parents.

Taxi driver: Hello, where are you going?
WANG Dali: Hello, we'd like to go to Gulou Street.
Xiaolong: Dad, did you live on Gulou Street before?
WANG Dali: Yes. I lived there with your grandparents before I went to America.
Xiaofeng: Are we going to stay at Grandpa and Grandma's house?
WANG Dali: Yes.
Xiaofeng: Then where will Auntie Linda and Uncle ZHANG stay?
WANG Dali: They're staying at Great Wall Hotel. We'll go and meet them tomorrow.

Xiaolong (Looking out of the car window): Beijing has so many cars.
Xiaofeng: And so many bicycles.
WANG Dali: Do you know the Chinese words for these vehicles?
Xiaolong: I know the one we're taking now is called *chuzuche*. A bike is *zixingche*. That's all the names I know.
WANG Dali: Truck is *kache*. The Chinese word for bus is *bashi*. You can also call it *gonggong qiche*.
Xiaolong: Oh, I see. All the vehicles in Chinese use the word "*che*".
WANG Dali: Exactly. In Chinese, "take a taxi" is also called *da che*.
Xiaolong: *Da*? Beat? It's so funny. Why would they want to "beat a taxi"?
WANG Dali: Haha… Actually it's not "beat a taxi." The word "*da*" has many meanings in Chinese. *Da dianhua* means "make a phone call," not "beat the phone." *Da che* means "take a taxi".
Xiaolong: *Da che*… I got it.

Xiaofeng: When will we get there?
WANG Dali: Soon. Look! Here we are. This is my home.
Driver: The fare is 87 *kuai*.
WANG Dali: Here's 90 *kuai*.
Driver: Here's your change, 3 *kuai*. Be sure to take all your things with you and don't leave anything behind.
WANG Dali: Thank you. We're finally home.

奇妙中国游

MAGICAL TOUR OF CHINA

# 第五集
# 见到爷爷奶奶

Chapter 5
Meeting Grandpa and Grandma

# 第五集　见到爷爷奶奶
…… Meeting Grandpa and Grandma

# 第五集　见到爷爷奶奶
…… Meeting Grandpa and Grandma

## 课文 Text

# 第五集　见到爷爷奶奶

刚下出租车，王大力一家就看见两位老人已经在门口等候他们了。

王大力：爸、妈，我们都回来了！
李美兰：爸、妈，你们好！等好久了吧？小龙、小凤，快叫爷爷、奶奶！
小龙，小凤：爷爷好！奶奶好！
爷　　爷：你们好！欢迎！欢迎！太好了，都回来了！
奶　　奶：小龙，小凤，快来让奶奶看看！
小　　龙：爷爷，您的房子真好看。
小　　凤：在美国没有这样的房子。

爷　　爷：这叫"四合院"，只有中国才有。
奶　　奶：好了，快进屋里休息吧！以后再慢慢看。
李美兰：爸、妈，您身体还好吧？
奶　　奶：挺好的。
小　　龙：爷爷奶奶家的电视好大呀！
奶　　奶：哎呀！你们要回来，我们特地去买的呀！
小龙、小凤：谢谢爷爷奶奶！
爷　　爷：没想到小龙小凤的中文说得那么好！
小　　龙：当然喽！爸爸妈妈一直教我们呢！

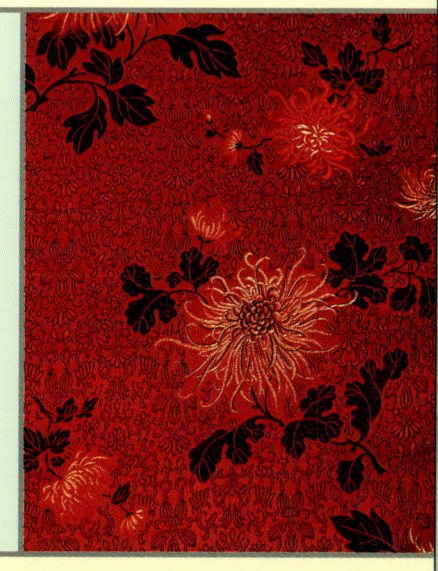

李美兰：小龙、小凤，你们给爷爷奶奶的礼物呢？
小龙、小凤：哦，差点忘了！
小　　凤：奶奶，这是我送给您的礼物。
　　　　　这是我的相册，都是我最喜欢的相片。
小　　龙：我也有礼物，看！这是我画的！
爷爷、奶奶：你画的是谁啊？
小　　龙：啊？我画的是爷爷奶奶呀！不像吗？
爷　　爷：哈哈哈…像，当然像！

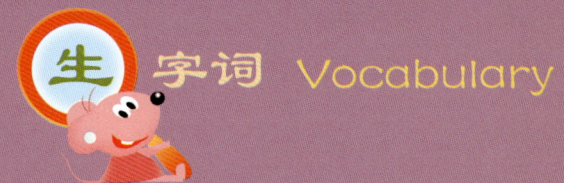

## Vocabulary

| | | |
|---|---|---|
| 刚 | gāng | just |
| 门口 | mén kǒu | doorway |
| 等候 | děng hòu | to wait |
| 回来 | huí lai | to return |
| 好看 | hǎo kàn | good looking |
| 这样 | zhè yàng | in this way |
| 四合院 | sì hé yuàn | traditional Chinese house with courtyard in the center flanked by living quarters on three sides and an enclosed wall in front |
| 只有 | zhǐ yǒu | only |
| 进 | jìn | to enter |
| 屋 | wū | house, room |
| 挺 | tǐng | fairly, quite |
| 特地 | tè dì | specially |
| 教 | jiāo | to teach |
| 差点 | chà diǎn | almost, a little bit short |
| 相册 | xiàng cè | photo album |
| 相片 | xiàng piàn | photograph |
| 像 | xiàng | similar to |

饭馆一景
A local restaurant

## 语法 Grammar

### 刚...就...

"刚...就" means the second action takes place right after the first action.

小龙刚坐下，电话就响了。
As soon as Xiaolong sits down, the phone rings.

小凤刚回家，朋友就来找她玩儿了。
As soon as Xiaofeng got home, her friend came to play with her.

### 只有...才...

"Only if...then...", the second part is dependent on the first.

只有在北京，才能吃到地道的北京烤鸭。
Only in Beijing can we have authentic Peking Duck.

只有中国才有大熊猫。
Only in China can we find the Giant Panda.

### 是...的

This structure is used to signify possession or can contain a verb to show who is performing the action.

这个布娃娃是 Ruby 的。
This rag doll belongs to Ruby.

那扇窗户是 David 打开的。
It's David who opened the window.

北海公园御膳堂
*The Imperial Dining Room* in *Bei Hai Park*

## 练习例句　Sample exercises

（一）Please rewrite the following sentences with "只有…才".

◆ 例句：夏天5点之前起床，能看到日出。
　　　　夏天只有5点之前起床，才能看到日出。

1. 王老先生觉得自己种菜，能有吃不完的菜。
　_____

2. 那种水果很特别，在他的家乡有。
　_____

3. 这个题很难写，老师会，同学们都不会。
　_____

（二）In China, how would you address the following people?

| | |
|---|---|
| 爸爸、妈妈的朋友，男，姓王，比爸爸大 | |
| 奶奶的朋友，女，姓张 | |
| 你的同学，女，叫小文 | |
| 你的老师，男，姓李 | |
| 妈妈的朋友，女，叫美兰 | |

## 说文解字
## Chinese Characters

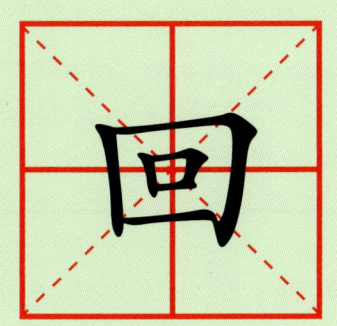

在中国古代，"回"字的样子看起来就像池塘里面水的漩涡。漩涡里的水转来转去，所以"回"的本义就是旋转。后来，"回"字的写法变化了，意思也变成了"返回"。我们常说的"回家"里的"回"就是这个意思。想一想，我们每天早上去上学，晚上又回家，像不像漩涡里的水，转来转去呢？

### 生字词

| | | |
|---|---|---|
| 池塘 | chí táng | pond |
| 本义 | běn yì | original meaning |
| 变化 | biàn huà | to change |
| 返回 | fǎn huí | to return, come back |

| | | |
|---|---|---|
| 漩涡 | xuàn wō | swirl |
| 旋转 | xuán zhuǎn | to circle |
| 变成 | biàn chéng | to turn into |

## 妙语如珠 Words & Phrases

### lǐ shàng wǎng lái
### 礼尚往来
"Courtesy goes back and forth."
People treat others the way they are treated.

### lǐ duō rén bú guài
### 礼多人不怪
"The very courteous are never blamed."
If you are very polite, people won't say bad things about you.

有一天，小龙正在写作业，小凤走过来，对他说："小龙，我不会写礼物的'礼'字。你教教我吧？"小龙正在忙着写作业，说："烦死了，等一下告诉你。"小凤："不嘛，你现在就告诉我吧。"妈妈听见了，说："小龙小凤，你们都不对，小龙没有讲礼貌，小凤没有讲道理。小龙，妹妹对你有礼貌，你也要对妹妹有礼貌。小凤，哥哥在忙，你要等哥哥忙完了再帮助你。虽然你有了礼貌，但是没有考虑哥哥在忙，也是不讲道理的。"

中国人讲"礼"是因为它在中国文化当中的地位十分重要。别人对你有礼貌，你也要对别人有礼貌，国家之间也是这样。后来"礼"也有了礼物的意思，别人送给你礼物你也要送给别人礼物。对别人有礼貌，总是好的。即使礼貌多了一些，别人也不会责怪。这就叫"礼多人不怪"。

礼是中国文化的核心，人的行为都要"有礼"，人与人之间的关系都有"礼"来规范。中文里有很多与"礼"有关的词语，像"敬礼"、"礼节"、"礼仪"、"礼物"、"典礼"。古代的中国曾经被称为"礼仪之邦"。

### 生字词

| 忙 | máng | busy |
| 烦 | fán | annoying |
| 礼貌 | lǐ mào | courtesy |
| 核心 | hé xīn | core |
| 敬礼 | jìng lǐ | to salute |
| 礼节 | lǐ jié | etiquette |
| 礼仪 | lǐ yí | protocol |
| 典礼 | diǎn lǐ | ceremony |

我们可以这样说：
① 礼尚往来是我们的好传统。
It is our tradition to be polite with each other.

② 国家与国家之间也要礼尚往来。
Nations also operate under protocols with each other.

③ 去看朋友多带点礼物吧，礼多人不怪嘛。
You should bring gifts when visiting your friends, because respect will always be appreciated.

# 华夏文化
# Chinese Culture

## 送礼的习惯

外国朋友在中国送礼，先要弄清楚，可以送什么，不可以送什么。如果送了不合适的礼物，就会闹笑话了。

在中国，白色和黑色常常代表不吉利。所以，在包礼物时，可不要用白色或黑色的包装纸。给中国老人送礼，一定不要送钟表，因为"送钟"听起来就像"送终"，意思是"给长辈办丧事"。给夫妻送礼不要送梨，因为"梨"听起来就像分离的"离"。这都很不吉利。

外国朋友收到礼物时，习惯当面打开看。中国人正相反，他们会等客人走了以后，再打开礼物。因为他们觉得当面打开礼物是不礼貌的。所以，如果你送礼物给中国朋友，而他没有当面打开，你可不要误会，这是因为习惯不同。不过，习惯是会变的。现在，有很多中国年轻人在收到礼物时，也会当面打开。

## 生字词

| 外国 | wài guó | foreign country |
| 弄清楚 | nòng qīng chǔ | to make clear |
| 合适 | hé shì | appropriate |
| 礼物 | lǐ wù | gift, present |
| 闹笑话 | nào xiào hua | to do something stupid or embarrassing |
| 不吉利 | bù jí li | inappropriate |
| 包 | bāo | to pack |
| 包装纸 | bāo zhuāng zhǐ | wrapping paper |
| 钟表 | zhōng biǎo | clocks and watches |
| 送终 | sòng zhōng | to bury a person, to go to someone's funeral |
| 丧事 | sāng shì | funeral affairs, funeral arrangements |
| 离 | lí | to separate |
| 收到 | shōu dào | to receive |
| 当面 | dāng miàn | before somebody's eyes |
| 正相反 | zhèng xiāng fǎn | just the opposite |
| 客人 | kè rén | guest |
| 误会 | wù huì | to misunderstand |

### Giving Gifts

Gift giving is an important part of Chinese culture, and Chinese people will generally bring some kind of gift whenever they visit friends. There are lots of traditions associated with giving gifts as well, which are important to take into account. For example, it is considered unlucky to give four of anything, because of the similarity between the Chinese words for "Four" and "Death".

## Dì wǔ jí  Jiàn dào yéye nǎinai

Gāng xià chūzūchē, Wáng Dàlì yìjiā jiù kànjiàn liǎng wèi lǎorén yǐjīng zài ménkǒu děnghòu tā men le.

Wáng Dàlì: Bà, mā, wǒmen dōu huílai le!
Lǐ Měilán: Bà, mā, nǐmen hǎo! Děng hǎo jiǔle ba? Xiǎolóng, Xiǎofèng, kuài jiào yéye, nǎinai!
Xiǎolóng, Xiǎofèng: Yéye hǎo! Nǎinai hǎo!
Yéye: Nǐmen hǎo! Huānyíng! Huānyíng! Tàihǎo le, dōu huílai le!
Nǎinai: Xiǎolóng, Xiǎofèng, kuài lái ràng nǎinai kànkan!
Xiǎolóng: Yéye, nín de fángzi zhēn hǎokàn.
Xiǎofèng: Zài Měiguó méiyǒu zhèyàng de fángzi.
Yéye: Zhè jiào "sìhéyuàn", zhǐyǒu Zhōngguó cái yǒu.
Nǎinai: Hǎo le, kuài jìn wū lǐ xiūxi ba! Yǐhòu zài mànmān kàn.

Lǐ Měilán: Bà, mā, nín shēntǐ hái hǎo ba?
Nǎinai: Tǐng hǎo de.
Xiǎolóng: Yéye nǎinai jiā de diànshì hǎo dà ya!
Nǎinai: āiyā! Nǐmen yào huílai, wǒmen tèdì qù mǎi de ya!
Xiǎolóng, Xiǎofèng: Xièxie yéye nǎinai!
Yéye: Méi xiǎng dào Xiǎolóng Xiǎofèng de Zhōngwén shuō de nàme hǎo!
Xiǎolóng: Dāngrán lou! Bàba māma yìzhí jiāo wǒmen ne!
Lǐ Měilán: Xiǎolóng, Xiǎofèng, nǐmen gěi yéye nǎinai de lǐwù ne?
Xiǎolóng, Xiǎofèng: O, chàdiǎn wàng le!
Xiǎofèng: Nǎinai, zhè shì wǒ sònggěi nín de lǐwù. Zhè shì wǒde xiàngcè, dōu shì wǒ zuì xǐhuan de xiàngpiàn.
Xiǎolóng: Wǒ yě yǒu lǐwù, kàn! Zhè shì wǒhuà de!
Yéye, Nǎinai: Nǐhuà de shì shuí a?
Xiǎolóng: á? Wǒhuà de shì yéye nǎinai ya! Bú xiàng ma?
Yéye: Hā hā hā...xiàng, dāngrán xiàng!

我送你一个礼物.

谢谢你! 你太客气了.

## Chapter 5: Meeting Grandpa and Grandma

(When they get out of the taxi, WANG Dali's family see that Grandpa and Grandma are already waiting at the gate.)

WANG Dali: Dad, Mom, we're here.
LI Meilan: Hello, Dad! Hello, Mom! Have you been waiting long? (To the children) Xiaolong, Xiaofeng, say hello to Grandpa and Grandma.
Xiaolong, Xiaofeng: Hello, Grandpa. Hello, Grandma.
Grandpa: Hello. Welcome. It's so nice that you're all here.
Grandma: How you've grown!
Xiaolong: (Looking around) Grandpa, your house is so nice.
Xiaofeng: There aren't these kinds of houses in America.
Grandpa: This is called a "*Si he yuan*". Only China has this kind of house.
Grandma: Come in and rest up first. You can have a look later.

LI Meilan: Dad, Mom, how are you?
Grandma: We're fine. You should take care of yourselves in the US, too.
Xiaolong: Grandma's TV is so big.
Grandma: Oh, we bought it just before you came back.
Xiaolong, Xiaofeng: Thank you, Grandpa and Grandma.
Grandpa (to WANG Dali): I didn't expect that Xiaolong and Xiaofeng could speak such good Chinese.
Xiaolong: Of course. Mom and Dad have been teaching us all along.
LI Meilan: Xiaolong, Xiaofeng, don't you have presents for Grandpa and Grandma?
Xiaolong, Xiaofeng: Oh, we almost forgot.
Xiaofeng: Grandma, this is my present for you. It's my photo album with all my favorite photos in it.
Xiaolong: I also have a present for you—Look! I drew it myself.
Grandpa & Grandma: Who are they?
Xiaolong: They are Grandpa and Grandma. Doesn't it look like you?
Grandpa: Haha. Yes, of course it does.

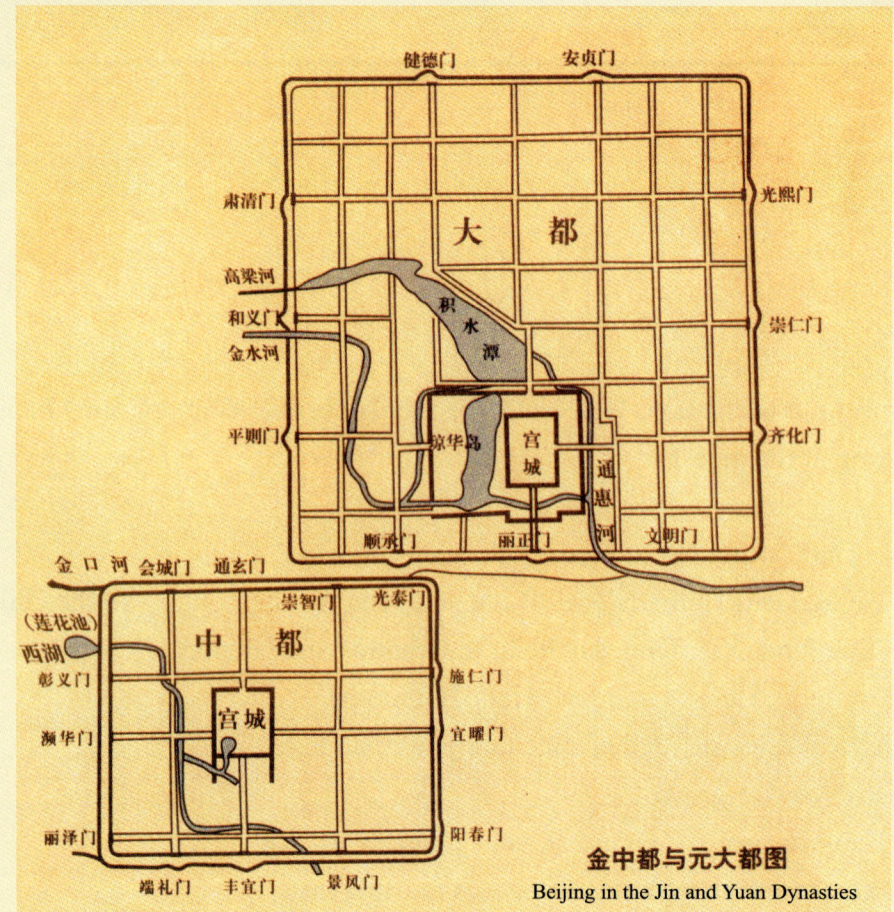

金中都与元大都图
Beijing in the Jin and Yuan Dynasties

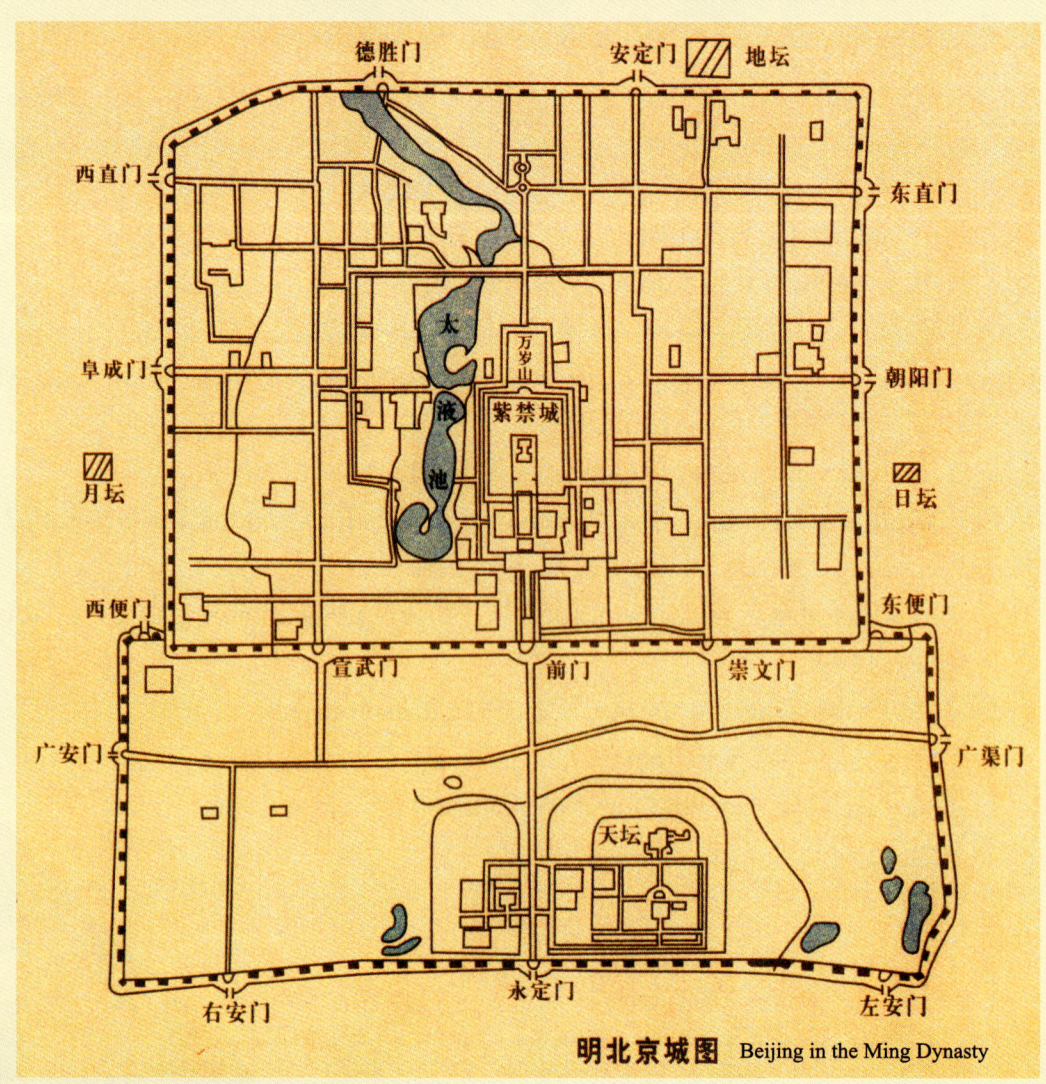

明北京城图　Beijing in the Ming Dynasty

# 第六集
# 水饺还是睡觉？

Chapter 6
*Shuǐjiǎo* Or *Shuìjiào?*

# 第六集 水饺还是睡觉?
…… Shuǐjiǎo Or Shuìjiào?

您好!欢迎来到长城饭店。

您好,两家人,订了四间房。

好的。请先填一下这张表格。

这个饭店真大,真漂亮!

看起来很棒哦!一定很贵。

请问,这里 shuǐ jiǎo 一晚多少钱?

水饺?小朋友,你得到餐厅里去问问。

什么?餐厅?

## 课文  Text

### 第六集  水饺还是睡觉？

张华一家和Smith一家来到了长城饭店。

服务员：您好！欢迎来到长城饭店。
Linda：您好，两家人，订了四间房。
服务员：好的。请先填一下这张表格。

你知道中国的历史有多长吗？

嗯...好像有5000多年。

David：这个饭店真大，真漂亮！
Jason：看起来很棒哦！一定很贵。
David：请问，这里 shuǐ jiǎo 一晚多少钱？
服务员：水饺？小朋友，你得到餐厅里去问问。
David：什么？餐厅？
Linda：哈哈哈... David，你把睡觉说成水饺了！水饺是dumpling. 你不能说"睡一晚多少钱"，你应该说"住一晚多少钱"，懂吗？

Jason：哈哈哈..."Night"和"bowl"在中文里发音是一样的，都是wǎn。
David：水饺一碗？睡觉一晚？哈哈哈...
Jason：It's so funny!
David：Jason，你忘了要扣分吗？
Jason：哦，我是说，太有趣了！中文真好玩！
David：我学会说水饺了。等一下我就要吃一碗水饺！

茶壶  Teapot

 生字词 Vocabulary

| | | |
|---|---|---|
| 服务员 | fú wù yuán | waiter, waitress, receptionist |
| 订 | dìng | to reserve |
| 间 | jiān | [a measure word for rooms] |
| 表格 | biǎo gé | form |
| 把...当成 | bǎ...dāng chéng | to take [something] as [something] |
| 发音 | fā yīn | pronunciation |
| 碗 | wǎn | bowl |

水饺　Dumplings

# 语法 Grammar

## …起来

"起来" used with verbs to indicate a subjective judgment, such as "look/listen/smell/taste+起来".

她看起来很漂亮。他看起来很帅。
She looks very pretty. He looks very handsome.

这朵花闻起来很香。
This flower smells very fragrant.

## 得

"得" can mean "to receive" or be used as a particle indicating a description of an action.

① 得 (dé) to get, to gain, to receive.
她得了第一名。
She came in first.
他得到一份礼物。
He received a gift.

② 得 (de) It can be put between a verb and an adjective to describe an action.
他跳得高。
He jumps high.

她饭吃得很慢。
She eats the food very slowly.

③ 得 (děi) means "have to, need to".
很晚了，我得马上走了。
It's very late. I have to go now.

张华明天早上五点就得起床，所以他今天晚上得早点儿睡觉。
ZHANG Hua has to get up at five o'clock tomorrow morning, so he must go to sleep earlier tonight.

## 看/听/说+成

to see/hear/speak...incorrectly as...

你把小明看成大中了。
You mistake Xiaoming as Dazhong.

你把"王"写成"玉"了。
You wrote "Wang" instead of "Yu".

## 中文的同音词 Homophones

In Chinese, like in English, some words with different meanings have the same pronunciation. These are called homophones.

"唐代"和"糖袋"都读"táng dài"。
Tang Dynasty and "bag of sugar" are both pronounced "táng dài".

"公园"和"公元"都读"gōng yuán"。
"Garden" and "A.D." are both pronounced "gōng yuán".

"大钟"和"大中"都读"dà zhōng"。
Big bell, and the name "Dazhong" are both pronounced "dà zhōng".

## 练习例句 Sample exercises

（一）What would you say in the following situations?

◆ 例句：来到饭店要住宿，对服务员说：<u>我要一间房间</u>。

1. 在餐厅，想知道一个菜是多少钱，对服务员说：_____。

2. 没有听清楚别人说的话，可以说：_____。

3. 住饭店之前想知道房间的价钱，对服务员说：_____。

（二）Use "起来" to complete the following sentences:

◆ 例句：文文，个子，看，高
　　　　文文个子看起来很高。

1. 华华，跳，远
   _____

2. 爸爸，字，写，快
   _____

3. 妹妹，声音，听，好听
   _____

4. 那条路，看，长
   _____

东苑戏楼
Dong Yuan Opera Hall

## 说文解字
## Chinese Characters

　　"睡"字有两部分。左边是"目",就是眼睛。右边是"垂",是"低下"的意思。这两部分在一起,就像"低着头,闭着眼打瞌睡"。慢慢地,这个字的意思就变成了"睡觉"。

　　很多跟眼睛有关的字里面都有一个"目"字。比如看东西要用眼睛,所以"看"字里面就有个"目"字。还有"眼睛"这两个字里都有"目"字。想一想,还有哪些字有"目"字?

### 生字词

| | | |
|---|---|---|
| 目 | mù | eye |
| 低下 | dī xià | to let droop |
| 打瞌睡 | dǎ kē shuì | to nap, to doze |
| 比如 | bǐ rú | for example |

| | | |
|---|---|---|
| 垂 | chuí | to hang down |
| 闭 | bì | to shut, to close |
| 慢慢地 | màn mān de | slowly |

## 妙语如珠 Words & Phrases

### mǎ ma hū hū
### 马马虎虎

"Horse horse tiger tiger." This is used to mean "so-so" or "not great", and can be used as a response to questions like "How are you?".

　　David 不小心，把"睡觉"说成了"水饺"。如果一个人做事情不认真，像 David 一样，我们可以说：这个人做事真马虎，或者这个人做事马马虎虎的。

　　马和虎在一起为什么就是不认真的意思呢？原来很久以前一个画家画画不认真。他画的马像虎，画的虎像马。谁也不知道他画的是什么，所以大家都说他画的是"马虎"。从此以后，人们就用"马虎"、"马马虎虎"来形容那些做事情不认真的人。

　　但是"马虎"和"马马虎虎"的意思不完全一样。"马马虎虎"除了有不认真的意思以外，还有"just so-so"的意思。如果有人问你："最近身体怎么样？"你可以说："马马虎虎，还可以吧。"

### suí suí biàn biàn
### 随随便便

This expression means "careless" or "lackadaisical".

　　A："你想吃什么？"
　　B："随便。"
　　这是我们常常听到的对话。"随便"就是"It doesn't matter to me; Whatever is easy"的意思。"随便"和"随随便便"的意思不同。

　　"随随便便"是不认真，马虎的意思，"随便"没有这个意思。

　　如果有人询问你的意见，但是你没有什么好主意，就可以说："随便。"但是不能说"随随便便"。

　　"你想喝什么？""随便。""你想看什么书？""随便。""我们去哪里玩？""随便。"

　　"随便"这个词很好用，但是如果说多了，别人可能会觉得没有意思。

### hú shuō bā dào
# 胡说八道

"Tartars speak 8 times." This means "nonsense" and is an example of how in the past the Chinese could look down on outsiders.

中国古代称呼亚洲中部、西部和南部一些民族为"胡人",他们说的话中国人听不明白,所以"胡说"就是听不明白的话。"八道"是指胡人写的文字、笔画。这些文字中国人也看不明白。所以"胡说八道"意思就是nonsense。别人说的话完全不对的时候,你可以说:"胡说八道。"或者"别胡说八道了。"

比如:
"听说你参加学校的篮球队了?"
"别胡说八道了。我根本不会打篮球。"
"胡说八道"对亲密的朋友可以用,但是对其他人说就有点不礼貌。

**生字词**

| | | |
|---|---|---|
| 不小心 | bù xiǎo xīn | incautious |
| 画家 | huà jiā | painter |
| 认真 | rèn zhēn | careful |
| 马虎 | mǎ hu | careless |
| 从此以后 | cóng cǐ yǐ hòu | from now on |
| 形容 | xíng róng | describe |
| 完全 | wán quán | completely |
| 一样 | yí yàng | same |

| | | |
|---|---|---|
| 随便 | suí biàn | to do as one pleases |
| 对话 | duì huà | dialogue, conversation |
| 询问 | xún wèn | to ask |
| 意见 | yì jian | suggestion, opinion |
| 民族 | mín zú | ethnicity |
| 胡人 | hú rén | Tartars |
| 亲密 | qīn mì | intimate |

富贵平安
New Year's painting -
"Prosperity and Peace"

# 华夏文化
# Chinese Culture

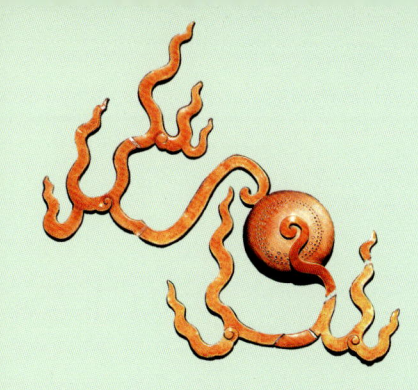

## 中文的谐音

在中文里，有些字的读音一样或者很像。比如"水饺"和"睡觉"；"一碗"和"一晚"。这就叫谐音。

中文里有很多谐音，比如"四"和"死"，"八"和"发"；所以中国人很喜欢数字八，不喜欢四。

有些谐音还和中国人的习俗有很大关系。过春节时，人们喜欢贴年画。年画上经常画着鱼。"鱼"和"余"读音一样。过年贴上画着鱼的画，就叫"年年有余(鱼)"。意思是生活好，每年的食物都吃不完。有的年画上画着蝙蝠，因为"蝙蝠"的"蝠"和"幸福"的"福"发音相同。还有桔子，因为"桔"和"吉祥"的"吉"发音很像，颜色也很亮丽，所以人们过年时常吃桔子，送礼也会送桔子。苹果也是好礼物，因为"苹"和"平安"的"平"发音一样。

还有些字人们不喜欢，所以，跟它们读音一样的字就成了忌讳。第5课我们学的"送钟"和"送终"，"梨"和"离"都是这样的。

### 生字词

| 谐音 | xié yīn | partial tone |
| 读音 | dú yīn | pronunciation |
| 习俗 | xí sú | custom |
| 关系 | guān xi | personal connection, relationship |
| 贴 | tiē | to paste |
| 年画 | nián huà | Chinese New Year Pictures |
| 余 | yú | surplus |
| 食物 | shí wù | foods |
| 蝙蝠 | biān fú | bat |
| 幸福 | xìng fú | happiness |
| 忌讳 | jì huì | taboo |

## Homophones

Chinese has lots of homophones, or words that have the same sounds. In some instances, you can differentiate the words by their tones, such as "shui jiao" (dumplings) and "shui jiao" (sleep). Other times, words will have the same pronunciation and tone, but are represented by different characters, such as "you" (also) and "you" (right).

## Dìliù jí Shuǐjiǎo háishì shuìjiào?

Zhāng Huá yìjiā hé Smith yìjiā lái dào le Chángchéng Fàndiàn.

Fúwùyuán: Nín hǎo! Huānyíng lái dào chángchéng fàndiàn.
Linda: Nín hǎo, liǎng jiārén, dìng le sì jiān fáng.
Fúwùyuán: Hǎode. Qǐng xiān tián yí xià zhè zhāng biǎogé.

David: Zhè ge fàndiàn zhēn dà, zhēn piàoliang!
Jason: Kànqǐlái hěn bàng o! Yídìng hěn guì.
David: Qǐngwèn, zhèlǐ shuǐjiǎo yìwǎn duōshǎoqián?
Fúwùyuán: Shuǐjiǎo? Xiǎo péngyou, nǐ děi dào cāntīng lǐ qù wènwen.
David: Shénme? Cāntīng?
Linda: Hāhāhā... David, nǐ bǎ shuìjiào shuōchéng shuǐjiǎo le! Shuǐjiǎo shì dumpling. Nǐ bù néng shuō "shuì yìwǎn duōshǎoqián", nǐ yīnggāi shuō "zhù yìwǎn duōshǎoqián", dǒng ma?
Jason: Hā hā hā... "night" hé "bowl" zài Zhōngwén lǐ fāyīn shì yíyàng de, dōu shì wǎn.
David: Shuǐjiǎo yìwǎn? Shuìjiào yìwǎn? Hā hā hā...
Jason: It's so funny!
David: Jason, nǐ wàng le yào kòu fēn ma?
Jason: Ò, wǒ shì shuō, tài yǒuqù le! Zhōngwén zhēn hǎowán!
David: Wǒ xué huì shuō shuǐjiǎo le. Děngyíxià wǒ jiù yào chī yì wǎn shuǐjiǎo!

故宫一景　　Roofs of the Forbidden City

# Chapter 6: *Shuǐjiǎo* or *Shuìjiào?*

The ZHANGs and the Smiths arrive at the Great Wall Hotel.

(At the reception desk)
The clerk: Hello! Welcome to the Great Wall Hotel.
Linda: Hello, we're two families with a reservation for four rooms.
The clerk: OK. Please fill in this form.


Jason and David look around the hall.
David: This hotel is so big and so beautiful.
Jason: It looks really great. It must be very expensive.
David (to the clerk): Excuse me, *zheli shuǐjiǎo(shuijiào) yi wan duoshao qian?*
The clerk: *Shuǐjiǎo?* Young man, you'll have to ask at the restaurant.
David: What? Restaurant?
Linda: Haha... David, you said *shuǐjiǎo* instead of *shuijiào*. *Shuǐjiǎo* is dumpling. You don't ask *shuijiao yi wan duo shao qian*, you say *zhu yi wan duo shao qian*, understand?
Jason: Haha, night and bowl are both pronounced *wan* in Chinese.
David: *Shuǐjiǎo yi wan? Shuìjiào yi wan?* A bowl of dumplings? Sleep one night? Hahaha...
Jason: It's so funny.
David: Jason, did you forget about taking off points?
Jason: Oh, I mean *tai youqu le*. Chinese is so interesting.
David: Anyway, now I know how to say dumpling in Chinese. I'm going to have some *shuijiao* tonight.

故宫太和殿飞檐：
图中右边第一个是骑凤仙人，后面跟着神话中的十个动物，传说它们能消灾灭祸、战胜邪恶。
Statuettes on the corner of the rooftop represent mythical animals which are said to have the power to dispel evil, avert misfortune and uphold justice. Only the buildings where the emperor resided could have nine or more such statuettes.

# 第七集
# 姑妈还是姨妈？

Chapter 7
Paternal Auntie or Maternal Auntie?

# 第七集 姑妈还是姨妈？
…… Paternal Auntie or Maternal Auntie?

奶奶，我想看看这张大照片，可以吗？

当然可以！正好可以认认亲戚。

这是你们的叔叔，这是你们的姑妈和姑父，

这是你们的表弟元元。

叔叔就是uncle吧？

对！

那姑妈一定是auntie喽！

没错。表弟就是姑妈的儿子。

我在美国也有表弟，Alan是我美国姑妈的儿子！

不对，你在美国的auntie是你的姨妈。

姨妈？姑妈？不都是auntie吗？

# 第七集 姑妈还是姨妈？
…… Paternal Auntie or Maternal Auntie?

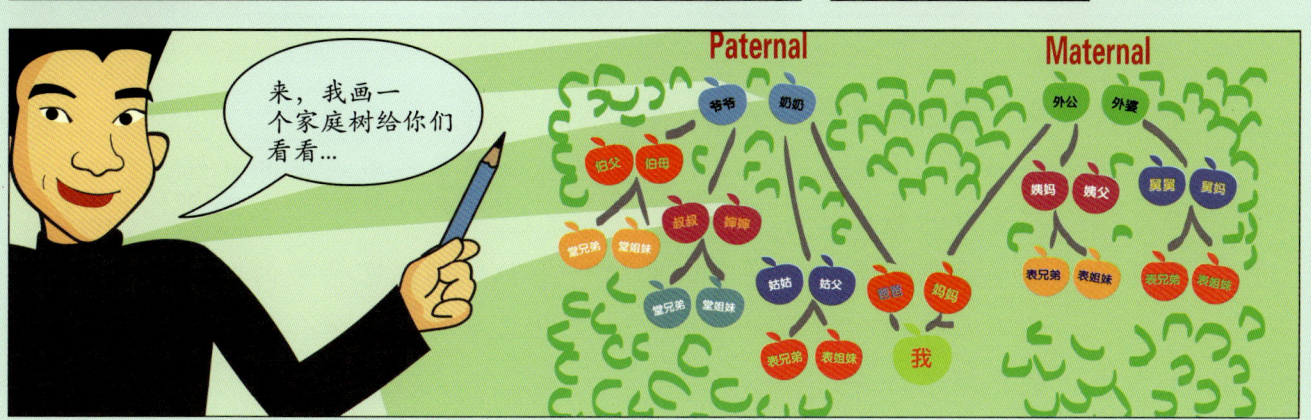

## 课文 Text

### 第七集 姑妈还是姨妈？

小　龙：奶奶，我想看看这张大照片，可以吗？
奶　奶：当然可以！正好可以认认亲戚。这是你们的叔叔，这是你们的姑妈和姑父，这是你们的表弟元元。
小　龙：叔叔就是uncle吧？
王大力：对！
小　凤：那姑妈一定是auntie喽！

王大力：没错。表弟就是姑妈的儿子。
小　龙：我在美国也有表弟，Alan是我美国姑妈的儿子！
李美兰：不对，你在美国的auntie是你的姨妈。
小　龙：姨妈？姑妈？不都是auntie吗？
王大力：Auntie在英文里没有区别，在中文里可不同啊！姨妈是妈妈的姐妹，姑妈是爸爸的姐妹。还有，中文里uncle也不同呀！爸爸的哥哥叫伯伯，爸爸的弟弟叫叔叔，妈妈的哥哥和弟弟都叫舅舅...

小　龙：噢！爸爸你好像在说绕口令。
小　凤：我知道！小龙是我的哥哥，不是我的弟弟。我是他的妹妹，不是他的姐姐。
李美兰：对了，中文里对爸爸家亲戚的叫法和对妈妈家亲戚的叫法是不一样的。唉！慢慢来，这些中文名称可要学一阵子的！
小　龙：我真搞不清楚！
王大力：来，我画一个家庭树给你们看看...

 Vocabulary

| | | |
|---|---|---|
| 姑妈 (爸爸的姐妹) | gū mā | paternal auntie |
| 姨妈 (妈妈的姐妹) | yí mā | maternal auntie |
| 认 | rèn | to get to know, to recognize |
| 亲戚 | qīn qi | relatives |
| 姑父 | gū fu | paternal aunt's husband |
| 表弟 | biǎo dì | younger male cousin with different last name |
| 区别 | qū bié | difference, to tell apart |
| 可 | kě | so, such (emphasis) |
| 姐妹 | jiě mèi | sisters |
| 伯伯 (爸爸的哥哥) | bó bo | father's elder brother |
| 舅舅 (妈妈的哥哥或弟弟) | jiù jiu | mother's brother |
| 好像 | hǎo xiàng | as if, like |
| 绕口令 | rào kǒu lìng | tongue twister |
| 叫法 | jiào fǎ | called, way of addressing |
| 唉 | ài | [a groaning sound] |
| 名称 | míng chēng | name, title |
| 一阵子 | yí zhèn zi | a while |
| 搞 | gǎo | to do, to work |
| 清楚 | qīng chǔ | to be clear about, understand |
| 家庭 | jiā tíng | family |

这就是中国的"泥人".

英语是 mud figurine.

## 语法 Grammar

### Verb+一阵子

"V+一阵子" means that the action in the verb will take a while.

以前常常看到她，但她有一阵子没来了。
She was usually seen occasionally, but she hasn't come here for some time.

这些书够你看一阵子的。
It will take you a while to read through all these books.

### 可

This can be used as an intensifying adverb, meaning "so" or "such".

学好中文可要一阵子的！
It will take you a while to learn Chinese.

她这人可好了！
She is such a nice person.

### 正好

正好 has two meanings. One meaning is "just right", the other is "by chance".

① just right

这双鞋我穿正好。
This pair of shoes fits me well.

秋天不热也不冷，正好出去旅游。
Autumn is neither hot nor cold—just the right time for traveling.

② by chance

我们正好要去超市。
We happen to go to the supermarket.

我要还小文书，正好在操场遇到她。
I wanted to return the book to Xiaowen and I happened to see her on the playground.

### 没错和不错

① While answering the affirmative, 没错 is the same as 不错。

不错，她是我的学生。
Right, she is my student.

没错，她是我的学生。
Correct, she is my student.

② But only "不错" has the meaning of "not bad; pretty good".

他英语学得不错,还懂得一点法语。
His English is very good, and he knows a little French.

这家饭馆的菜做得不错。
The food in the restaurant is pretty good.

## 练习例句　Sample exercises

（一）Make sentences with 好像。

◆ 例句：今天一天小龙都没怎么说话，好像生病了。

1. 早上天上就有乌云，好像_____
2. 她妹妹的头发长长的，眼睛大大的，好像_____
3. _____，好像_____

（二）Please use ...也... to rewrite the following sentences:

◆ 例句：　Jason 是 Linda 和 Mike 儿子。
　　　　　Jason 是 Linda 的儿子，也是 Mike 的儿子。

1. 气球有蓝色的和黄色的。
   _____

2. 我星期三和星期五上中文课。
   _____

3. Ruby和小凤会打乒乓球。
   _____

皇城艺术馆
Huang Cheng Art Museum

# 说文解字
## Chinese Characters

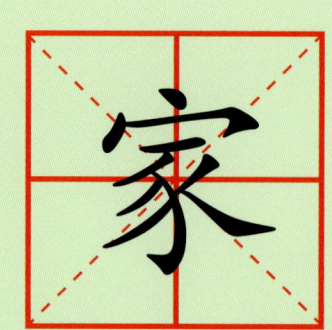

　　除了"象形"和"形声"两种造字法以外，中文造字的第三种方法是"会意"（compounds）。它是把两个或两个以上的字合在一起说一个新的意思。"家"就是会意字。"宀"(mián)是屋顶，在这里指房子。"豕"（shǐ）是猪。在古代，中国人每家都会养猪，因为多数中国人吃的肉主要是猪肉。有屋子有食物，人才可以住下，这就是"家"。人们住在房子里组成"家庭"。

　　中文造字的最后一种方法是指事，就是在图形上加上一些符号来表示意义的造字法。如"本"字，它是在"木"字下加了一个"一"，表示树根。

　　中文用象形和指事这两种方法造出来的字常常是比较简单的，只有一个部分组成；而形声和会意造出来的字有两个或两个以上的部分组成。

### 生字词

| | | |
|---|---|---|
| 会意 | huì yì | compounds |
| 新 | xīn | new |
| 屋顶 | wū dǐng | roof |
| 养 | yǎng | to raise |
| 猪肉 | zhū ròu | pork |
| 食物 | shí wù | food |
| 指事 | zhǐ shì | a way of creating new Chinese characters from existing characters |
| 图形 | tú xíng | figure |
| 符号 | fú hào | symbol, sign |

## 妙语如珠 Words & Phrases

dǎ pò shā guō wèn dào dǐ
### 打破砂锅问到底

"The crack goes to the bottom of the clay pot." To ask questions persistently until one gets to the bottom of the things.

今天华语老师教 David"口"就是"嘴巴"的意思。David 回家后，对 Jason 说："你看，'口'字长得多像一张嘴巴呀，所以，'口'就是'嘴巴'的意思。"Jason 问 David："口是一张嘴巴，那'回'的意思就是两张嘴巴了？"David 回答不出来，就说："你怎么那么多问题呀？"Jason 说："对不明白的事，当然要打破砂锅问到底了。"

打破砂锅问到底，原来是说打破砂锅"纹"到底。砂锅破了，上面会有裂纹，这个裂纹会一直到砂锅的底，我们要看个明白。因为纹和问的读音相近，现在写成"问"，意思也变成：对不明白的事情，一定要问个明白。

### 生字词

| 回答 | huí dá | to answer |
| 问题 | wèn tí | question |
| 对 | duì | for, of |
| 明白 | míng bai | to understand |

我们还可以这样说：

① David 对汉字不太明白。他最怕 Jason 打破砂锅问到底了。
David is not very clear about Chinese characters, so he is afraid that Jason will persist in asking him questions.

② 我们学中文的时候，可要打破砂锅问到底。
When we are learning Chinese, we should know the exact answer to the question and the reason behind it.

③ 华华喜欢问问题，把问题弄明白，总是不停地问，真是打破砂锅问到底啊！
Huahua likes to keep asking questions about things she doesn't understand, and she won't stop until she gets to the bottom of things.

你怎么那么多问题？

对，我就是喜欢"打破砂锅问到底"。

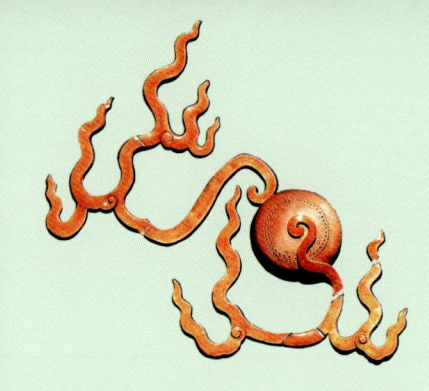

# 华夏文化
# Chinese Culture

## 中国传统家庭

中国对亲属的称谓比较讲究。每个人的称谓代表了他在家庭里的地位，正确地称呼家庭里的每一个人是中国礼仪的一部分。

爸爸的爸爸叫"爷爷"。爸爸的妈妈是"奶奶"。妈妈的爸爸，在中国的北方叫"姥爷"，在中国的南方叫"外公"。妈妈的妈妈在中国的北方叫"姥姥"，在中国的南方叫"外婆"。

爸爸的哥哥叫"伯伯"，弟弟叫"叔叔"，爸爸的姐妹是"姑姑"。妈妈的兄弟是"舅舅"，妈妈的姐妹是"姨妈"。伯伯和叔叔的孩子是我的堂亲，要叫他们"堂哥""堂弟""堂姐""堂妹"；姑姑、姨妈和舅舅的孩子是我的表亲，要叫他们"表哥""表弟""表姐""表妹"。

因此，每个人在家庭里的关系通过他们之间的称呼变得很清楚，一定不会出错。

### 生字词

| | | |
|---|---|---|
| 亲属 | qīn shǔ | relative |
| 称谓 | chēng wèi | form of address |
| 讲究 | jiǎng jiū | particular, specific |
| 代表 | dài biǎo | to represent |
| 地位 | dì wèi | status, specific place |
| 礼仪 | lǐ yí | etiquette |
| 一部分 | yí bù fen | a part of |
| 姥爷、外公 | lǎo ye, wài gōng | maternal grandfather |
| 姥姥、外婆 | lǎo lao, wài pó | maternal grandmother |
| 伯伯 | bó bo | elder uncle |
| 兄弟 | xiōng dì | brother |
| 堂亲 | táng qīn | cousin with the same family name |
| 表亲 | biǎo qīn | cousin with different family name |

## Chinese Family

In Chinese there are many more descriptive terms for family members than in English. Each person has his/her specific place in the family hierarchy. Chinese people don't merely say Uncle, they also specify paternal or maternal and whether the Uncle is older or younger than their parents.

## Dìqī jí  Gūmā háishi yímā?

Xiǎolóng: Nǎinai, wǒ xiǎng kànkan zhè zhāng dà zhàopiàn, kěyǐ ma?

Nǎinai: Dāngrán kěyǐ! Zhènghǎo kěyǐ rènren qīnqi. Zhè shì nǐmen de shūshu, zhè shì nǐmen de gūmā hé gūfu, zhè shì nǐmen de biǎodì yuányuán.

Xiǎolóng: Shūshu jiù shì uncle ba?

Wáng Dàlì: Duì!

Xiǎofèng: Nà gūmā yídìng shì auntie lou!

Wáng Dàlì: Méicuò. Biǎodì jiù shì gūmā de érzi.

Xiǎolóng: Wǒ zài Měiguó yě yǒu biǎodì, Alan shì wǒ Měiguó gūmā de érzi!

Lǐ Měilán: Búduì, nǐ zài Měiguó de auntie shì nǐ de yímā.

Xiǎolóng: Yímā? Gūmā? Bú dōu shì auntie ma?

Wáng Dàlì: Auntie Zài Yīngwén lǐ méiyǒu qūbié, zài Zhōngwén lǐ kě bùtóng a! Yímā shì māma de jiěmèi, gūmā shì bàba de jiěmèi. Háiyǒu, Zhōngwén lǐ uncle yě bùtóng ya! Bàba de gēge jiào bóbo, bàba de dìdi jiào shūshu, māma de gēge hé dìdi dōu jiào jiùjiu...

Xiǎolóng: ō! Bàba nǐ hǎoxiàng zài shuō ràokǒulìng.

Xiǎofèng: Wǒ zhīdao! Xiǎolóng shì wǒde gēge, bú shì wǒde dìdi, wǒ shì tāde mèimei, bú shì tāde jiějie.

Lǐ Měilán: Duì le, Zhōngwén lǐ duì bàba jiā qīnqi de jiàofǎ hé duì māma jiā qīnqi de jiàofǎ shì bùyíyàng de. ài! Mànmān lái, zhèxiē Zhōngwén míngchēng kě yào xué yízhènzi de!

Xiǎolóng: Wǒ zhēn gǎo bù qīngchu!

Wáng Dàlì: Lái, wǒ huà yíge jiātíng shù gěi nǐmen kànkan...

# Chapter 7: Paternal Auntie or Maternal Auntie

Xiaolong (points to the photo on the wall): Grandma, is it okay to look at this photo?

Grandma (takes down the photo): Of course. It will be a good way to get to know your relatives. This is your *shūshu*, and this is your *gūmā* and *gūfu*. This is your *biǎodì* Yuanyuan.

Xiaolong: *Shūshu* is uncle, right?

WANG Dali: Right.

Xiaofeng: And *gūmā* must be auntie.

WANG Dali: Yes. *biǎodì* is the son of *gūmā*.

Xiaolong: I have a *biǎodì* in America, too. He's the son of my *gūmā* in the US.

LI Meilan: No, your auntie in the US is your *yímā*.

Xiaolong: *gūmā*? *yímā*? What's the difference?

WANG Dali: In English, there is only auntie, but it's quite different in Chinese. *Yímā* is the sister of your mother, while *gūmā* is the sister of your father. Uncle is also different in Chinese. We have *bóbo*, your father's elder brother, and *shūshu*, your father's younger brother. But both your mother's elder brother and younger brother are called *jiùjiu*...

Xiaolong: Oh, man. Dad, you're doing a tongue twister.

Xiaofeng: I know! Xiaolong is *gēge* because he is my older brother, and not my younger brother *dìdi*. I am *mèimei*, his younger sister, not his *jiějie*.

LI Meilan: Right, in Chinese we have different words for maternal relatives and paternal relatives. Let's take it slowly—it will take you a while to learn all these names.

Xiaolong: It's so confusing.

WANG Dali: Come, let me draw a family tree to show you...

北海白塔，建于公元1651年。
White Dagoba in *Bei Hai Park*

# 第八集
## 哪里，哪里

Chapter 8

*Nali, Nali*

# 第八集　哪里，哪里
…… Nali, Nali

# 第八集　哪里，哪里
……*Nali, Nali*

你说什么？
你慢点说好吗？

No — problem, No problem! 我说得对吗？

No — problem! 意思是"没问题"。

哪里！哪里！

很好！你说得很好。

哪里？嗯…你的发音很好。

哪里！哪里！

你为什么总问我"哪里"啊？我已经回答你了。

嗯？啊！我明白了！我不是在问你"哪里"。你刚刚不是夸我英语说得好吗？我说"哪里"的意思是说…嗯…我英语说得不太好。

啊？！

你说得很好呀！为什么要说不好呢？

爸爸妈妈说有礼貌的孩子要谦虚，不能骄傲。人家夸奖我，我就得说"哪里，哪里"，才有礼貌。大人也一天到晚说"哪里，哪里"，对不对？

哦…我又搞不清楚了！

## 课文 Text

## 第八集 哪里，哪里

晚上，姑妈带着小龙的表弟元元来了。

姑妈： 你们好！
小龙，小凤： 姑妈好！
元元： 你们好！我叫元元。
小龙： 你好，我叫小龙。
小凤： 我叫小凤，元元哥哥好！
元元： 哇！你们的汉语说得很棒嘛！我还以为你们只会说英语呢！昨天我学了一个晚上怎么用英语打招呼，还怕你们听不懂呢！

小凤： 慢点！请你说慢点！你说的"hang you"（汉语）是什么？我已经听不懂了。
元元： "汉语"，哦！就是中国话，也就是华语，你们是说Chinese, 对吧？以后我可以教你们说华语，你们也可以教我说英语，OK？
小龙： No problem!
元元： 你说什么？你慢点说好吗？
小龙： No —— problem! 意思是"没问题"。
元元： No —— problem, No problem! 我说得对吗？
小龙： 很好！你说得很好。
元元： 哪里！哪里！

小龙： 哪里？嗯...你的发音很好。
元元： 哪里！哪里！
小龙： 你为什么总问我"哪里"啊？我已经回答你了。
元元： 嗯？啊！我明白了！我不是在问你"哪里"。你刚刚不是夸我英语说得好吗？我说"哪里"的意思是说...嗯...我英语说得不太好。
小龙，小凤： 啊？！
小龙： 你说得很好呀！为什么要说不好呢？
元元： 爸爸妈妈说有礼貌的孩子要谦虚，不能骄傲。人家夸奖我，我就得说"哪里，哪里"，才有礼貌。大人也一天到晚说"哪里，哪里"，对不对？
小龙： 哦...我又搞不清楚了！

#  Vocabulary

| | | |
|---|---|---|
| 汉语 | hàn yǔ | Chinese |
| 嘛 | ma | [an ending word for a rhetorical question] |
| 以为 | yǐ wéi | to think, to believe, to consider |
| 打招呼 | dǎ zhāo hu | say hello |
| 怕 | pà | afraid |
| 话 | huà | word, language |
| 问题 | wèn tí | question, problem |
| 总 | zǒng | always |
| 回答 | huí dá | to answer |
| 明白 | míng bai | to understand |
| 刚刚 | gāng gāng | just now |
| 夸 | kuā | to praise |
| 礼貌 | lǐ mào | politeness |
| 谦虚 | qiān xū | modest, humble |
| 骄傲 | jiāo ào | be proud |
| 人家 | rén jiā | other people |
| 夸奖 | kuā jiǎng | to praise |
| 大人 | dà rén | adult, grown-up |
| 一天到晚 | yì tiān dào wǎn | day to night |

古代的鼎，用于祭祀。
Ancient *Ding*, a ceremonial container

## 语法 Grammar

### "总" 和 "一直"

"总" and "一直" both have the meaning of "always". "一直" indicates an uninterrupted action or a constant state, while "总" indicates an action repeats regularly.

他从9点到12点一直在做作业。
He has been doing his homework from 9 to 12 o'clock.

他来北京总要吃烤鸭。
He always has Peking Duck when he comes to Beijing.

### 教

"教" means "to teach" and has two pronunciations.

① 教 (jiāo) means "to teach".

你可以教我英语啊!
You may teach me English.

教我做中国菜吧!
Please teach me how to cook Chinese food.

② 教 (jiào) is a word element.

教师 teacher
教材 teaching material

### 问题

"问题" not only means question, but also means "problem", "trouble" and "difficulty" in Chinese.

① question

这个问题不好回答。
This question is hard to answer.

你能回答我的问题吗?
Can you answer my question?

② problem

你可以帮我吗?     没问题!
Can you help me?   No problem!

③ trouble

我的电脑出问题了。
There is something wrong with my computer.

### Verb+得+不+adjective

The negative form of V+得+adj: Verb+得+不+adjective.

小龙说得不对。
What Xiaolong said was not correct.

雨下得不大。
It's not raining hard.

## 练习例句　Sample exercises

（一）Make sentences with 要说。

◆例句：　人家夸奖你，你要说：<u>"哪里，哪里。"</u>

1. 不小心踩了人家一下，要说：_____

2. 人家帮了你时，要说：_____

3. 人家跟你说不好意思，你要说：_____

4. _____，要说：_____

（二）Please use ...只...不... to rewrite the following sentences:

◆例句：　他们会说中文，也会说英文。
　　　　　<u>他们只会说中文，不会说英文。</u>

1. 小明爱看书也爱看报纸。
_____

2. Ruby上法语课也上舞蹈课。
_____

3. David喜欢猫也喜欢狗。
_____

4. 他们爱唱歌也爱跳舞。
_____

5. 小文吃冰淇淋也吃饼干。
_____

你最喜欢北京的什么地方？

嗯..我好多地方还没有去呢.

## 说文解字
## Chinese Characters

古代美女图　A painting of ancient beauty

　　"要"可以读yāo，它的本义是腰。腰在身体的中间位置，作用很大，所以"要"还可以读yào，意思是"重要"。我们可以这样记住这个字："要"的上边是"西施"的"西"，下边是"女"。西施是中国古代最美丽的女子，有很多人追求。所以"要"又有"求、取"的意思。

### 生字词

| | | |
|---|---|---|
| 腰 | yāo | waist |
| 身体 | shēn tǐ | body |
| 位置 | wèi zhi | position |
| 重要 | zhòng yào | important |
| 追求 | zhuī qiú | chase |

| | | |
|---|---|---|
| 西施 | xī shī | one of the 4 most beautiful women from Ancient China |
| 求 | qiú | to demand |
| 取 | qǔ | to fetch |

## 妙语如珠 Words & Phrases

没问题 — No problem.
没事儿 — No problem, it's not a issue.

不好意思 — I'm sorry, I feel embarrassed.
没关系 — It doesn't matter.

故宫一角
A shot of the *Forbidden City*

"能帮我个忙吗？""没问题！"
"对不起，我来晚了！""没关系。"
"不好意思，我今天有事，不能去了。""没事儿。"
没问题，没关系，没事儿，不好意思，这几个词很常用。
在回答别人的请求时，常常说："没问题！"
"没关系"和"没事儿"的意思差不多，在接受别人的歉意时常用。"没事儿"比"没关系"更口语化和随便。
"不好意思"这个词有几种意思。一种是害羞或者碍于面子不想做一件事，比如："我想请我的中国邻居教我中文，但是我不好意思问他"，"中文老师当着大家的面说我很聪明，我感到很不好意思"。有的时候，"不好意思"和"对不起"的意思差不多，表示歉意时经常会这么说，例如："不好意思，我还有别的事，得先走了"，"又让你请客，真不好意思"。

### 生字词

| 常用 | cháng yòng | in common use, frequently used |
| 请求 | qǐng qiú | request, to request |
| 接受 | jiē shòu | to accept |
| 歉意 | qiàn yì | apology, regrets |
| 口语化 | kǒu yǔ huà | oral |
| 随便 | suí biàn | as you like |
| 害羞 | hài xiū | be shy |
| 面子 | miàn zi | face |
| 邻居 | lín ju | neighbor |

我们还可以这样说：

① "星期天去打球，好吗？"
　　Let's play ball on Sunday, okay?

　"没问题！"
　　No problem.

② "我身体不舒服，不能和你一起去打球了。"
　　I am not feeling so well. I can't play ball with you.

　"没关系，你好好休息吧。"
　　It doesn't matter, have a rest.

③ "我忘了帮你买东西了。"
　　I forgot to buy your stuff.

　"没事儿，我自己去买吧。"
　　It's ok. I will buy them myself.

④ "不好意思，我现在没空。你可以等我一会儿吗？"
　　Sorry, I have no time now. Could you please wait for a while?

　"没问题！"
　　No problem.

⑤ "对不起，踩到你的脚了！"
　　Sorry, I stepped on your foot.

　"没事儿。"
　　Never mind.

⑥ "不好意思，借过！"
　　Excuse me, let me pass.

请你带我去爬长城好吗？

没问题！

# 华夏文化
## Chinese Culture

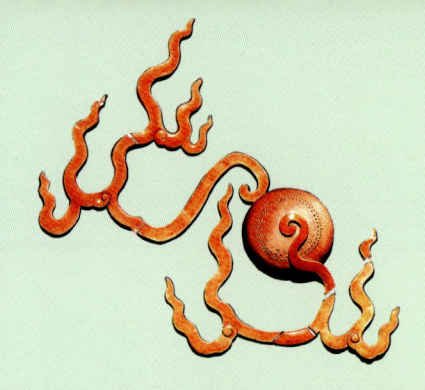

## 打招呼和告别

中国人与熟人、朋友见面时，爱问对方"吃了吗？"这么问表示亲热与关心，但西方人很少会问别人"Have you eaten?"小辈见到长辈要主动"叫人"，如"叔叔好，阿姨好！"在路上遇见朋友时，如果离得很远，不方便打招呼，我们也要向对方点点头，表示礼貌。在跟朋友说话时，我们会看着他的眼睛，表示我们在很认真地听。

告别时，中国人会和西方人一样说"再见"，客人走的时候主人还会说"您走好"，"慢走"。英语里类似的说法是"Take care"。

### 生字词

| | | |
|---|---|---|
| 表示 | biǎo shì | to show |
| 亲热 | qīn rè | intimate |
| 小辈 | xiǎo bèi | younger member of a family |
| 不方便 | bù fāng biàn | inconvenient |
| 点点头 | diǎn dian tóu | to nod |
| 认真 | rèn zhēn | earnest |
| 您走好 | nín zǒu hǎo | go safely |
| 慢走 | màn zǒu | walk slowly |
| 类似 | lèi sì | similar |

## 赞扬

在受到别人夸奖、赞扬时,中国人常常说"哪里,哪里","您过奖了"。这些话不是责怪或不相信夸赞的人,而是表示谦虚。现在中国的年轻人在别人夸奖时,也会像西方人一样说"谢谢"。

### 生字词

| | | |
|---|---|---|
| 您过奖了 | nín guò jiǎng le | You give me too much credit. |
| 夸赞 | kuā zàn | to praise |
| 责怪 | zé guài | to blame |
| 不相信 | bù xiāng xìn | do not believe |
| 年轻人 | nián qīng rén | youth |

### Modesty

Chinese people put a great emphasis on modesty, so when receiving compliments it is best to be humble and not appear overly proud. Chinese people will frequently respond to praise by saying "not really" or "it isn't so" and downplaying their achievement. It is considered crude to outright accept praise.

# Dìbā jí  Nǎli nǎli

Wǎnshang, gūmā dài zhe Xiǎolóng de biǎodì Yuányuán lái le.

Gūmā: Nǐmen hǎo !
Xiǎolóng, Xiǎofèng: Gūmā hǎo!
Yuányuán: Nǐmen hǎo! Wǒ jiào Yuányuán.
Xiǎolóng: Nǐhǎo, wǒ jiào Xiǎolóng.
Xiǎofèng: Wǒ jiào Xiǎofèng, Yuányuán gēge hǎo!
Yuányuán: Wa! Nǐmen de Hànyǔ shuō de hěn bàng ma! Wǒ hái yǐwéi nǐmen zhǐ huì shuō Yīngyǔ ne! Zuótiān wǒ xué le yíge wǎnshang zěnme yòng Yīngyǔ dǎzhāohu, hái pà nǐmen tīng bù dǒng ne!
Xiǎofèng: Màn diǎn! Qǐng nǐ shuō màn diǎn! Nǐshuōde "hang you" (Hànyǔ) shì shénme? Wǒ yǐjīng tīng bù dǒng le.
Yuányuán: "Hànyǔ", ò! Jiù shì Zhōngguó huà, yě jiù shì huáyǔ, nǐmen shì shuō Chinese, duì ba? Yǐhòu wǒ kěyǐ jiāo nǐmen shuō huáyǔ, nǐmen yě kěyǐ jiāo wǒ shuō Yīngyǔ, OK?
Xiǎolóng: No problem!
Yuányuán: Nǐ shuō shénme? Nǐ màn diǎn shuō hǎo ma?
Xiǎolóng: No——problem! Yìsi shì "méi wèntí".
Yuányuán: No—— problem, No problem! Wǒ shuō de duì ma?
Xiǎolóng: Hěnhǎo! Nǐshuōde hěnhǎo .
Yuányuán: Nǎli! Nǎli!
Xiǎolóng: Nǎli? ng … nǐ de fāyīn hěnhǎo.
Yuányuán: Nǎli! Nǎli!
Xiǎolóng: Nǐ wèishénme zǒng wèn wǒ "nǎli" a? Wǒ yǐjīng huídá nǐ le.
Yuányuán: ng? à ! Wǒ míngbai le! Wǒ bú shì zài wèn nǐ "nǎli". nǐ gānggāng bú shì kuā wǒ Yīngyǔ shuō de hǎo ma? Wǒ shuō "nǎli" de yìsi shì shuō…ng…Wǒ Yīngyǔ shuō de bú tài hǎo.
Xiǎolóng, Xiǎofèng: á？！
Xiǎolóng: Nǐ shuō de hěnhǎo ya! Wèishénme yào shuō bù hǎo ne?
Yuányuán: Bàba māma shuō yǒu lǐmào de háizi yào qiānxū, bù néng jiāo'ào. Rénjiā kuājiǎng wǒ, wǒ jiù děi shuō "nǎli, nǎli", cái yǒu lǐmào. Dàren yě yìtiāndàowǎn shuō "nǎli, nǎli", duìbuduì?
Xiǎolóng: ò…wǒ yòu gǎo bù qīngchu le!

# Chapter 8: *Nali, Nali*

In the evening, Guma and Yuanyuan come to Grandpa's home.

Guma: Hello.

Xiaolong, Xiaofeng: Hello, Guma.

Yuanyuan: Hello, my name is Yuanyuan.

Xiaolong: Hi, my name is Xiaolong.

Xiaofeng: My name is Xiaofeng. Hello.

Yuanyuan: Wow. Your Chinese is very good. I was expecting you to speak only English. Yesterday I practiced saying hello in English all night, and I was still afraid that you couldn't understand me.

Xiaofeng: Slowly, please speak slowly. What did you say in *hanyu* just now? I didn't catch it.

Yuanyuan: *Hanyu* is *Zhongguo hua*. You call it *huáyǔ*, right? Hey. I'll teach you Chinese, and you can teach me English, okay?

Xiaolong: No problem.

Yuanyuan: What? Would you please say it slowly?

Xiaolong: No——problem. It means *mei wenti*.

Yuanyuan: No——problem, no problem. Did I say it right?

Xiaolong: Very good. You said it very well.

Yuanyuan (bashfully): *Nali, nali.*

Xiaolong: Where? Um, your pronunciation is very good.

Yuanyuan (bashfully): *Nali, nali.*

Xiaolong: Why do you always ask me "where"? I've told you already!

Yuanyuan: Oh, I see. I didn't really mean "where." You praised my English just now, so I said *Nali, nali*. It means my English is not very good.

Xiaolong, Xiao Feng: What? Why?

Xiaolong: But you said it really well. Why do you say you didn't?

Yuanyuan: Dad and Mom say that a well-mannered person should be modest, not proud. Saying "*nali, nali*" is a way to be polite when others praise me. The adults say "*Nali, nali*" all the time, don't they?

Xiaolong: Hmm, I still don't get it. Chinese is sure confusing sometimes.

宫女图，明代唐寅画，藏于北京故宫博物院
Court ladies by *TANG Yin* of Ming Dynasty, *Beijing Palace Museum*

# 第九集
# 吃北京烤鸭

Chapter 9
Having Beijing Duck

# 第九集　吃北京烤鸭
…… Having Beijing Duck

嗨，Mike! 嗨，Linda! 昨晚睡得好吗?

还不错。见到你父母了?

是啊! 几乎一夜都没睡。

小龙和小凤也和表弟玩到好晚才睡，早上都起不来。后来一听说要和你们见面才起来的。

时差十多个小时，得要几天才调得过来。今天我们好好吃顿北京菜，好吗?

Sure! Dumplings anytime!

这还要感谢David呢!

太好了! 昨天晚上我们吃了一顿水饺。

David，扣一分! 你应该说中文。

哦! 我是说，我喜欢吃水饺。

北京的水饺最地道。

我们今天中午尝尝地道的北京烤鸭怎么样? 在北京吃北京烤鸭!

北京烤鸭! 北京烤鸭!

好主意!

# 第九集　吃北京烤鸭
······Having Beijing Duck

## 课文 Text

# 第九集 吃北京烤鸭

第二天中午，王大力一家来到了长城饭店与另外两家人一起吃午餐。

王大力：嗨，Mike! 嗨，Linda! 昨晚睡得好吗？
Linda: 还不错。见到你父母了？
王大力：是啊！几乎一夜都没睡。
李美兰：小龙和小凤也和表弟玩到好晚才睡，早上都起不来。后来一听说要和你们见面才起来的。
王大力：时差十多个小时，得要几天才调得过来。今天我们好好吃顿北京菜，好吗？
Linda: 太好了！昨天晚上我们吃了一顿水饺。
Jason: 这还要感谢 David 呢！

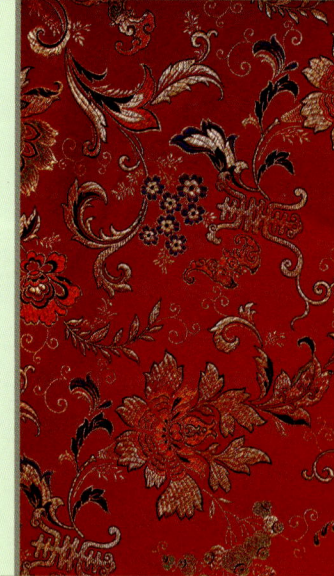

David: Sure! Dumplings anytime!
Linda: David, 扣一分！你应该说中文。
David: 哦！我是说，我喜欢吃水饺。
王大力：北京的水饺最地道。我们今天中午尝尝地道的北京烤鸭怎么样？在北京吃北京烤鸭！
David: 北京烤鸭！北京烤鸭！
Mike: 好主意！
张 华：David, Ruby! 你们今天也要学学怎么用筷子，昨天的水饺都是用刀叉吃的！
David: 筷子？哦，筷子太难用了。
Linda: 吃中国菜怎么能不用筷子呢？筷子不难用，练一练就会了。
王大力：小朋友，终于在北京吃到了北京烤鸭，跟美国的北京烤鸭比比看。
Ruby: 你们都吃过烤鸭，只有我没有吃过！

小 龙：Ruby, 你连烤鸭都没有吃过吗？
Ruby: 我在美国很少吃中餐。Joy 说上次吃烤鸭的时候我还是一个小婴儿呢！
王大力：没关系，Ruby, 我来教你传统的北京吃法：先拿一张饼，抹一点儿酱，放上烤鸭、葱丝和黄瓜，再卷起来，看！这样就可以了！
Ruby: 看起来很好吃哦！
小 龙：我记得在美国吃烤鸭的时候没有黄瓜呀！
王大力：这才是正宗的北京烤鸭啊！大家都来试试吧！
小 凤：天哪！David, 你的烤鸭掉到我的盘子里了！
David: 对不起！我也没办法，我用不好筷子。
Ruby: 爸爸，你帮我好不好？我什么都吃不到！
张 华：Ruby, 别着急！第一次用筷子都是这样的，以后就好了。
王大力：看来，这顿饭我们要慢慢吃了。

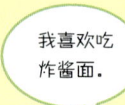

你喜欢吃烤鸭吗？

我喜欢吃炸酱面。

# 生字词 Vocabulary

| | | |
|---|---|---|
| 烤鸭 | kǎo yā | roast duck |
| 来到 | lái dào | to come to |
| 与 | yǔ | with |
| 另外 | lìng wài | other |
| 午餐 | wǔ cān | lunch |
| 昨晚 | zuó wǎn | last night |
| 几乎 | jī hū | almost |
| 夜 | yè | night |
| 后来 | hòu lái | afterwards |
| 见面 | jiàn miàn | to meet |
| 起来 | qǐ lái | to get up |
| 时差 | shí chā | time difference |
| 调 | tiáo | to adjust |
| 过来 | guò lái | to come over |
| 顿 | dùn | [a measure word for meals] |
| 感谢 | gǎn xiè | to thank |
| 筷子 | kuài zi | chopsticks |
| 刀 | dāo | knife |
| 叉 | chā | fork |
| 难 | nán | difficult |
| 练 | liàn | to practise |
| 连 | lián | even |
| 中餐 | zhōng cān | Chinese food |
| 传统 | chuán tǒng | traditional |
| 吃法 | chī fǎ | ways of eating |
| 饼 | bǐng | round flat cake |
| 抹 | mǒ | to brush |
| 酱 | jiàng | sauce |
| 放 | fàng | to put |
| 葱 | cōng | shallot |
| 丝 | sī | a thread |
| 黄瓜 | huáng guā | cucumber |
| 卷 | juǎn | to roll up |
| 记得 | jì de | remember |
| 正宗 | zhèng zōng | authentic |
| 试 | shì | to try |
| 掉 | diào | to fall down |
| 盘子 | pán zi | plate |
| 办法 | bàn fǎ | way to handle, method |
| 着急 | zháo jí | to worry |
| 看来 | kàn lái | seem |

 语法 Grammar

## 多

① many, much, more

超市里有很多苹果。
There are many apples in the supermarket.

Ruby有很多衣服。
Ruby has many clothes.

② (used after a number) more than, over

教室里有十多个人。
There are more than ten people in the classroom.

他五十多岁。
He is over 50.

③ used with "少", means "how many, how much"

这本书多少钱?
How much is that book?

书店有多少书?
How many books are there in the bookstore?

## 连...都...

This is close in meaning to "Doesn't ... even..."

连David也不知道成龙是谁吗?
Doesn't David even know who Jacky Chan is?

你连他也不认识吗?他是姚明。
Don't you even know him? He is YAO Ming.

## 跟

① to follow

小龙和小凤跟着爸爸和妈妈上了出租车。
Xiaolong and Xiaofeng get in a taxi with their parents.

他跟着她走了。
He followed her and left.

② Used to show comparison.

跟美国的北京烤鸭比比看。
Compare it with the Peking duck in the US.

她的书包跟我的书包不一样。
Her bag is different from mine.

农家一景
Window of a peasant home

## …起来

In Unit 6 we learned "Verb+起来" which indicated a subjective judgment. But here 起来 has a different meaning.

"起来" is used either after a verb or an adjective to express "up" or upward movement.

举起来 raise it up
拉起来 pull it up

## …怎么样？

① Means "How is…?"

今天天气怎么样？
What about the weather today?

今天下雨了。
It is raining.

那个饭馆的菜怎么样？
What about the food in that restaurant?

不错。
Quite good.

② Means "How about…?" is used to ask you whether you agree with the idea or not.

我们今天尝尝地道的烤鸭怎么样？
Shall we have some real Peking duck today?

好！
OK!

你星期日来我家玩怎么样？
How about coming to play at my place this Sunday?

对不起，我要去奶奶家。
Sorry, I am going to visit my Grandma.

## 练习例句　Sample exercises

（一）Use "好" or "好好" in the following sentences:

1. 今天我们要_____吃一顿。

2. 他是个_____孩子。

3. 雨下得_____大。

4. 今天妈妈不在家，你要_____的照顾妹妹。

5. _____一块表让他给弄坏了。

（二）Complete the following sentences:

◆例句：写完作业后，<u>我终于可以玩电脑游戏了。</u>

1. 放假了，我终于可以_____

2. 考完试，我终于可以_____

3. 来了中国，我终于可以_____

4. _____，我终于可以
_____

说文解字

Chinese Characters

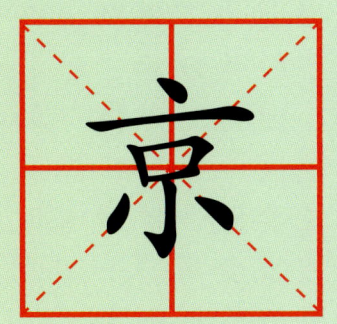

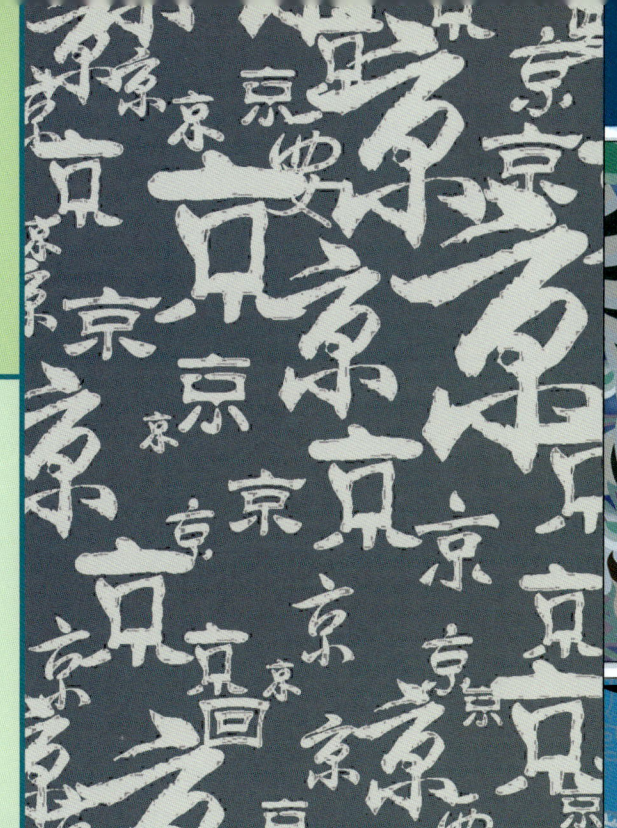

"京"是建在高台上的大房子。它的本义是高大的土丘，所以京就有高、大的意思。因为古代都城和国王的宫殿很多都建在高处，所以又把都城和宫殿在的地方叫作"京"。

### 生字词

| 建 | jiàn | to build |
| 高台 | gāo tái | terrace |
| 土丘 | tǔ qiū | mound |
| 都城 | dū chéng | capital |
| 宫殿 | gōng diàn | palace |

古玩店窗口
Window of an antique shop

## 妙语如珠 Words & Phrases

yī huí shēng, èr huí shóu
### 一回生，二回熟

"First time strange, second time familiar."
The more times you do something, the more skillful you become.

中国人爱吃米饭。第一次做米饭，可能会因为不熟练，而做出夹生饭。但有了经验以后，就能做出香香的熟饭了。因为"熟练"的熟和"熟饭"的熟是同一个字，而且意思也相近，所以在要做一件没有做过的事情时，人们常常会用"一回生，二回熟"来鼓励自己或别人。

**生字词**

| 生 | shēng | uncooked | 见面 | jiàn miàn | to meet, to come together |
| 熟 | shóu | cooked | 夹生饭 | jiā shēng fàn | half-cooked rice |
| 次数 | cì shù | times | 经验 | jīng yàn | experience |
| 越…越… | yuè… yuè… | the more…the more… | 相近 | xiāng jìn | closely, be closed to |
| 熟练 | shú liàn | skilled | 鼓励 | gǔ lì | to encourage |

我们还可以这样说：

① 第一次吃烤鸭卷不好饼没关系，"一回生，二回熟"，多卷几次就好了。
It is ok if you can't roll it up when you eat Peking duck the first time. Because the first time is strange, the second time familiar, the more you do it the better you will get.

② "一回生，二回熟"，多练习几次，你肯定就会用筷子了。
The first time is strange, the second time familiar, the more you use chopsticks the better you will get.

③ 你们两个刚认识，多见几次面就能一起聊天（chat）了，"一回生，二回熟"嘛！
You just met each other, and the more times you meet the more things you will get to talk about. As they say, "the first time is strange, the second time familiar."

## 华夏文化
## Chinese Culture

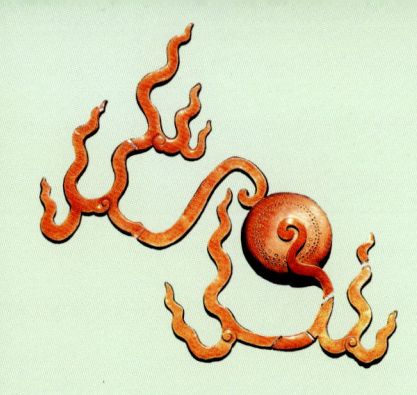

## 中国菜真好吃！

说到中国，就一定要说中国的美食。中国的农业一直很发达，古语说：民以食为天，意思是人们把"吃"看得比什么都重要。人们除了吃饱，还要吃好，于是就在做菜上下了很多功夫。

中国各个地区的菜肴都有特点。一般说来，四川菜、湖南菜比较辣，甚至很辣；广东菜讲究原汁原味，尤其是蔬菜、海鲜，更是要新鲜"生猛"；江浙菜细腻、山东菜味道浓厚。去餐馆的时候，喜欢吃辣的人，可以点宫爆鸡丁，麻婆豆腐等四川菜。喜欢甜味的人，可以点古老肉，松子鱼。想吃肉，有粉蒸排骨，鱼香肉丝，葱爆牛肉。鸡鸭类最有名的当然是北京烤鸭。想吃小吃，广东式（也有人说"港式"）点心很受欢迎，像虾饺、烧麦，在美国的许多超市都可以买到冷冻的。现做的水饺、拉面等北方点心在北京到处都见得到。

习惯上中国人喜欢大家围坐在一起，分享桌子上每一道菜，人多了可以吃到的美食种类就多些。一起吃饭比较热闹，大家有更多的机会沟通，彼此也容易更亲近一点儿。

## 生字词

| | | |
|---|---|---|
| 美食 | měi shí | delicious food |
| 农业 | nóng yè | agriculture |
| 发达 | fā dá | advance |
| 做菜 | zuò cài | cooking |
| 菜肴 | cài yáo | cuisine |
| 特点 | tè diǎn | characteristic |
| 辣 | là | spicy |
| 原汁原味 | yuán zhī yuán wèi | original juice and flavor |
| 海鲜 | hǎi xiān | seafood |
| 生猛 | shēng měng | proud, alive |
| 细腻 | xì nì | fine and smooth |
| 浓厚 | nóng hòu | strong |
| 宫爆鸡丁 | gōng bào jī dīng | spicy fried chicken cubes with peanuts (Kung Pao Chicken) |
| 麻婆豆腐 | má pó dòu fu | Spicy tofu (Ma Po Tofu) |
| 甜 | tián | sweet |
| 古老肉 | gǔ lǎo ròu | Sweet and Sour Pork |
| 松子鱼 | sōng zǐ yú | whole fish fried with pine nuts |
| 粉蒸排骨 | fěn zhēng pái gǔ | steamed ribs with rice |
| 鱼香肉丝 | yú xiāng ròu sī | fried pork strips with sweet and sour sauce |
| 葱爆牛肉 | cōng bào niú ròu | sliced beef fried with scallions |
| 烧麦 | shāo mài | a steamed dumpling with the dough gathered at the top |
| 冷冻 | lěng dòng | freeze |
| 沟通 | gōu tōng | to communicate |

## Chinese food is delicious

Chinese meals are much more communal than their Western counterpart. Dishes are shared, so more people means more of a chance to taste different and interesting foods. Of course, chopsticks are used instead of forks and knives, which can be tricky at first when dealing with small foods like peanuts, but with a little practice it becomes easy. Chinese food varies greatly between different places in China and there are lots of regional specialties to explore.

圆形玉龙
A dragon design in jade

## Dì jiǔ jí   Chī Běijīng kǎoyā

Dì'èr tiān zhōngwǔ, Wáng Dàlì yìjiā láidào le Chángchéng Fàndiàn yǔ lìngwài liǎng jiā rén yìqǐ chī wǔcān.

Wáng Dàlì: Hāi, Mike! Hāi, Linda! Zuówǎn shuì de hǎo ma?
Linda: Hái búcuò. Jiàndào nǐ fùmǔ le?
Wáng Dàlì: Shì a! Jīhū yí yè dōu méi shuì.
Lǐ Měilán: Xiǎolóng hé Xiǎofèng yě hé biǎodì wán dào hǎo wǎn cái shuì, zǎoshang dōu qǐbulái. Hòulái yì tīngshuō yào hé nǐmen jiànmiàn cái qǐlái de.
Wáng Dàlì: Shíchā shí duō gè xiǎoshí, děi yào jǐ tiān cái tiáo de guòlái. Jīntiān wǒmen hǎohao chī dùn Běijīng cài, hǎo ma?
Linda: Tài hǎo le! Zuótiān wǎnshang wǒmen chī le yí dùn shuǐjiǎo.
Jason: Zhè hái yào gǎnxiè David ne!
David: Sure! Dumplings anytime!
Linda: David, Kòu yìfēn! Nǐ yīnggāi shuō Zhōngwén.
David: ò! Wǒ shì shuō, wǒ xǐhuan chī shuǐjiǎo.
Wáng Dàlì: Běijīng de shuǐjiǎo zuì dìdào. Wǒmen jīntiān zhōngwǔ chángchang dìdào de Běijīng kǎoyā zěnmeyàng? Zài Běijīng chī Běijīng kǎoyā!
David: Běijīng kǎoyā! Běijīng kǎoyā!
Mike: Hǎo zhǔyi!
Zhāng Huá: David, Ruby! Nǐmen jīntiān yě yào xuéxue zěnme yòng kuàizi, zuótiān de shuǐjiǎo dōu shì yòng dāo chā chī de!
David: Kuàizi? O, kuàizi tài nán yòng le.
Linda: Chī Zhōngguócài zěnme néng bú yòng kuàizi ne? Kuàizi bù nán yòng, liàn yí liàn jiù huì le.
Wáng Dàlì: Xiǎo péngyou, zhōngyú zài Běijīng chī dào le Běijīng kǎoyā, gēn Měiguó de Běijīng kǎoyā bǐbi kàn.
Ruby: Nǐmen dōu chī guò kǎoyā, zhǐyǒu wǒ méiyǒu chī guò!
Wáng Xiǎolóng: Ruby, Nǐ lián kǎoyā dōu méiyǒu chī guò ma?
Ruby: Wǒ zài Měiguó hěn shǎo chī zhōngcān. Joy shuō shàng cì chī kǎoyā de shíhou wǒ háishì yíge xiǎo yīng'ér ne!
Wáng Dàlì: Méiguānxi, Ruby, wǒ lái jiāo nǐ chuántǒng de Běijīng chīfǎ: Xiān ná yì zhāng bǐng, mǒ yìdiǎnr jiàng, fàng shàng kǎoyā, cōngsī hé huángguā, zài juǎn qǐlai. Kàn! Zhèyang jiù kěyǐ le!
Ruby: Kànqǐlai hěn hǎochī o!
Wáng Xiǎolóng: Wǒ jìde zài Měiguó chī kǎoyā de shíhou méiyǒu huángguā ya!
Wáng Dàlì: Zhè cái shì zhèngzōng de Běijīng kǎoyā a! Dàjiā dōu lái shìshi ba!
Wáng Xiǎofèng: Tiān na! David, Nǐ de kǎoyā diào dào wǒde pánzi lǐ le!
David: Duìbuqǐ! Wǒ yě méi bànfǎ, wǒ yòngbuhǎo kuàizi.
Ruby: Bàba, nǐ bāng wǒ hǎobuhǎo? Wǒ shénme dōu chī bú dào!
Zhāng Huá: Ruby, bié zháojí! Dì yī cì yòng kuàizi dōu shì zhèyàng de, yǐhòu jiù hǎo le.
Wáng Dàlì: Kànlái, zhè dùn fàn wǒmen yào mànmān chī le.

# Chapter 9: Having Beijing Duck

The next day, the Wang Family go to the Great Wall Hotel to have lunch with the other two families.

WANG Dali: Hi, Mike. Hi, Linda. How did you sleep last night?
Linda: Not bad. You saw your parents?
WANG Dali: Yes. We stayed up all night talking.
LI Meilan: Xiaolong, Xiaofeng played with their cousin and did not go to bed until late. They didn't want to get up this morning, but when they heard that we were having lunch with you, they were up in no time.
WANG Dali: With more than ten hours' time difference, we'll need a few days to adjust. Shall we have real Beijing food today?
Lina: That would be great. The dumplings last night were delicious.
Jason: We should thank David for that.
David: Sure, dumplings anytime.
Linda: David, take off one point. You should speak Chinese.
David: Oh! I mean *wo xihuan chi shuijiao*.
WANG Dali: The dumplings in Beijing are the real thing. Shall we have some real Peking duck today? Peking duck in Peking!
David: Peking duck. Peking duck. *Beijing kaoya! Beijing kaoya.*
Mike: Good idea. *Hao zhuyi.*
ZHANG Hua: David, Ruby! You should learn to use chopsticks this time. You were using a fork and knife for the dumplings last night!
David: Chopsticks? Oh, no! It's too difficult.
Linda: How can you eat Chinese food without chopsticks? It's not difficult after you practice a little.

(The three families sit around the table, waiting for lunch)
WANG Dali: Kids, we are eating Peking duck in Beijing finally. You can compare it with the Peking duck in the US.
Ruby: You have all eaten Peking duck before, but not me.
Xiaolong: Ruby, haven't you ever eaten Peking duck before?
Ruby: I seldom have Chinese food in the US. Joy said the last time they had Peking duck was when I was a little baby.
WANG Dali: It's all right, Ruby, let me show you the traditional way to eat it. First, take a pancake, and then spread some sauce on it. Then put a few slices of duck, green onion, and some cucumber on the pancake. Now roll it up. There you go.
Ruby: It looks great.
Xiaolong: But I don't think there is cucumber with the Peking Duck in America.
WANG Dali: This is the authentic Peking Duck. Now try it yourselves.
Xiaofeng: My God. David, your duck fell onto my plate.
David: Sorry, I can't help it. I don't know how to use chopsticks well.
Ruby: Will you help me, Dad? I can't pick anything up.
ZHANG Hua: Take it easy. There is always a first time. You will get better at it after some practice.
WANG Dali: It looks like we're going to be taking this meal nice and slow.

静夜思　李白

床前明月光，
疑是地上霜。
举头望明月，
低头思故乡。

Before my bed a bright shade of light,
Almost take it as frost on the ground.
Looking up and finding the moon bright,
Lowering my head I long for my hometown.
by LI Bai, a famous poet of the Tang Dynasty

# 索引 INDEX

| 中文 | 拼音 | 英文 | 集 |
|---|---|---|---|
| **A** 阿姨 | ā yí | Auntie | 2 |
| 唉 | ài | [a groaning sound] | 7 |
| 安全带 | ān quán dài | seat belt | 3 |
| **B** 芭比 | bā bǐ | Barbie | 1 |
| 巴士 | bā shì | bus | 4 |
| 把…当成 | bǎ…dāng chéng | to take [something] as [something] | 6 |
| 办法 | bàn fǎ | way to handle, method | 9 |
| 榜样 | bǎng yàng | example, model | 1 |
| 边 | biān | [suffix, signifying direction] | 2 |
| 表弟 | biǎo dì | younger male cousin with different last name | 7 |
| 表格 | biǎo gé | form | 6 |
| 别 | bié | do not | 4 |
| 别的 | bié de | other | 2 |
| 饼 | bǐng | round flat cake | 9 |
| 伯伯 | bó bo | father's elder brother | 7 |
| 不错 | bú cuò | not bad, pretty good | 2 |
| 不好意思 | bù hǎo yì si | to feel shy or embarrassed (used as an apology) | 2 |
| **C** 才 | cái | [an adverb indicating that something has taken place later than usual or expected] | 3 |
| 叉 | chā | fork | 9 |
| 差不多 | chà bu duō | approximately, about | 3 |
| 差点 | chà diǎn | almost, a little bit short | 5 |
| 车 | chē | vehicle | 4 |
| 车费 | chē fèi | (taxi) fee | 4 |
| 成 | chéng | to become | 6 |
| 橙汁 | chéng zhī | orange juice | 3 |
| 吃法 | chī fǎ | ways of eating | 9 |
| 传统 | chuán tǒng | traditional | 9 |
| 次 | cì | time | 3 |
| 葱 | cōng | shallot | 9 |
| 错 | cuò | mistake, wrong | 4 |

| | | | | |
|---|---|---|---|---|
| **D** | 打车 | dǎ chē | to take a taxi | 4 |
| | 打鸡蛋 | dǎ jī dàn | to take the shell off an egg | 4 |
| | 打人 | dǎ rén | to beat someone | 4 |
| | 打招呼 | dǎ zhāo hu | say hello | 8 |
| | 打字 | dǎ zì | to type | 4 |
| | 大街 | dà jiē | street, avenue | 4 |
| | 大人 | dà rén | adult, grown-up | 8 |
| | 但是 | dàn shì | but | 2 |
| | 当然 | dāng rán | certainly, of course | 1 |
| | 刀 | dāo | knife | 9 |
| | 等候 | děng hòu | to wait | 5 |
| | 地道 | dì dào | authentic | 1 |
| | 掉 | diào | to fall down | 9 |
| | 订 | dìng | to reserve | 6 |
| | 懂 | dǒng | to understand | 2 |
| | 顿 | dùn | [a measure word for meals] | 9 |
| **E** | 儿子 | ér zi | son | 1 |
| **F** | 发音 | fā yīn | pronunciation | 6 |
| | 饭店 | fàn diàn | hotel | 4 |
| | 放 | fàng | to put | 9 |
| | 分数 | fēn shù | mark, score | 2 |
| | 凤 | fèng | phoenix | 1 |
| | 服务员 | fú wù yuán | waiter, waitress, receptionist | 6 |
| | 复活节 | fù huó jié | Easter | 1 |
| **G** | 感谢 | gǎn xiè | to thank | 9 |
| | 刚 | gāng | just | 5 |
| | 刚刚 | gāng gāng | just now | 8 |
| | 搞 | gǎo | to do, to work | 7 |
| | 告诉 | gào su | to tell | 1 |
| | 跟 | gēn | with, to follow | 4 |
| | 公共汽车 | gōng gòng qì chē | bus | 4 |
| | 姑父 | gū fu | paternal aunt's husband | 7 |
| | 姑妈 | gū mā | paternal auntie | 7 |
| | 鼓楼 | gǔ lóu | [a place in Beijing] | 4 |
| | 过来 | guò lái | to come over | 9 |
| **H** | 哈 | hā | ha [laughter] | 3 |
| | 嗨 | hāi | Hi, Hello | 2 |
| | 孩子 | hái zi | kid, child | 1 |
| | 汉语 | hàn yǔ | Chinese | 8 |

| | | | | |
|---|---|---|---|---|
| | 好看 | hǎo kàn | good looking | 5 |
| | 好消息 | hǎo xiāo xi | good news | 1 |
| | 好像 | hǎo xiàng | as if, like | 7 |
| | 好笑 | hǎo xiào | funny | 4 |
| | 后来 | hòu lái | afterwards | 9 |
| | 护照 | hù zhào | passport | 3 |
| | 话 | huà | word, language | 8 |
| | 黄瓜 | huáng guā | cucumber | 9 |
| | 回答 | huí dá | to answer | 8 |
| | 回来 | huí lai | to return | 5 |
| **J** | 几乎 | jī hū | almost | 9 |
| | 集合 | jí hé | to gather together | 2 |
| | 系 | jì | to tie, to buckle | 3 |
| | 记得 | jì de | remember | 9 |
| | 记住 | jì zhu | to remember | 2 |
| | 加 | jiā | to add | 3 |
| | 家庭 | jiā tíng | family | 7 |
| | 加州 | jiā zhōu | California | 3 |
| | 间 | jiān | [a measure word for rooms] | 6 |
| | 见面 | jiàn miàn | to meet | 9 |
| | 酱 | jiàng | sauce | 9 |
| | 教 | jiāo | to teach | 5 |
| | 骄傲 | jiāo ào | be proud | 8 |
| | 叫法 | jiào fǎ | called, way of addressing | 7 |
| | 结束 | jié shù | to finish | 2 |
| | 姐妹 | jiě mèi | sister | 7 |
| | 进 | jìn | to enter | 5 |
| | 进步 | jìn bù | (to make) progress | 1 |
| | 舅舅 | jiù jiu | mother's brother | 7 |
| | 卷 | juǎn | to roll up | 9 |
| **K** | 卡车 | kǎ chē | truck | 4 |
| | 开始 | kāi shǐ | to begin, to start | 2 |
| | 开心 | kāi xīn | happy, to have a good time | 1 |
| | 看来 | kàn lái | seem | 9 |
| | 烤鸭 | kǎo yā | roast duck | 9 |
| | 可 | kě | so, such (emphasis) | 7 |
| | 空中服务员 | kōng zhōng fú wù yuán | flight attendant | 3 |
| | 扣 | kòu | to deduct | 2 |
| | 夸 | kuā | to praise | 8 |

|   | 夸奖 | kuā jiǎng | to praise | 8 |
|---|---|---|---|---|
|   | 筷子 | kuài zi | chopsticks | 9 |
| **L** | 啦 | la | [ending word signifying emphasis] | 4 |
|   | 来到 | lái dào | to come to | 9 |
|   | 老公 | lǎo gōng | husband | 2 |
|   | 老样子 | lǎo yàng zi | (remain) the same | 2 |
|   | 落 | là | left out; missing | 4 |
|   | 礼貌 | lǐ mào | politeness | 8 |
|   | 连 | lián | even | 9 |
|   | 练 | liàn | to practise | 9 |
|   | 辆 | liàng | [a measure word for vehicles] | 4 |
|   | 另外 | lìng wài | other | 9 |
|   | 露营 | lù yíng | camping | 1 |
|   | 喽 | lou | [particle indicating the sentence is a statement] | 3 |
|   | 旅行 | lǚ xíng | to travel | 1 |
| **M** | 嘛 | ma | [ending word for a rhetorical question] | 8 |
|   | 马上 | mǎ shàng | right away | 3 |
|   | 麦当劳 | mài dāng láo | McDonald's | 1 |
|   | 慢慢 | màn mān | slowly | 1 |
|   | 忙 | máng | busy | 1 |
|   | 没 | méi | without, no | 4 |
|   | 没错 | méi cuò | right, correct | 4 |
|   | 门口 | mén kǒu | doorway | 5 |
|   | 明白 | míng bai | to understand | 8 |
|   | 名称 | míng chēng | name, title | 7 |
|   | 抹 | mǒ | to brush | 9 |
|   | 目的地 | mù dì dì | destination | 3 |
| **N** | 拿 | ná | to take | 4 |
|   | 那么 | nà me | so | 4 |
|   | 那样 | nà yàng | like that, that kind | 4 |
|   | 难 | nán | difficult | 9 |
|   | 哪儿 | nǎr | where | 4 |
|   | 嗯 | ng | uhm | 4 |
| **O** | 噢 | ò | oh [an exclamation] | 1 |
| **P** | 怕 | pà | afraid | 8 |
|   | 盘子 | pán zi | plate | 9 |
| **Q** | 奇妙 | qí miào | magical, wonderful | 3 |
|   | 其实 | qí shí | in fact, actually | 4 |

|   | 起飞 | qǐ fēi | to take off | 3 |
|---|---|---|---|---|
|   | 起来 | qǐ lái | to get up | 9 |
|   | 谦虚 | qiān xū | modest, humble | 8 |
|   | 亲戚 | qīn qi | relatives | 7 |
|   | 清楚 | qīng chǔ | to be clear about, understand | 7 |
|   | 请客 | qǐng kè | to invite | 2 |
|   | 区别 | qū bié | difference, to tell apart | 7 |
| R | 让 | ràng | to let | 2 |
|   | 绕口令 | rào kǒu lìng | tongue twister | 7 |
|   | 人家 | rén jiā | other people | 8 |
|   | 认 | rèn | to get to know, to recognize | 7 |
|   | 入境卡 | rù jìng kǎ | entry card | 3 |
| S | 时差 | shí chā | time difference | 9 |
|   | 试 | shì | to try | 9 |
|   | 叔叔 | shū shu | uncle (father's younger brother), a courteous way of addressing an older man | 1 |
|   | 输 | shū | to lose | 2 |
|   | 丝 | sī | a thread | 9 |
|   | 司机 | sī jī | driver | 4 |
|   | 四合院 | sì hé yuàn | traditional Chinese house with courtyard in the center flanked by living quarters on three sides and an enclosed wall in front | 5 |
|   | 所有 | suǒ yǒu | all | 4 |
| T | 太棒了 | tài bàng le | great, wonderful | 1 |
|   | 太太 | tài tai | Mrs.; wife | 2 |
|   | 特地 | tè dì | specially | 5 |
|   | 填写 | tián xiě | to fill in | 3 |
|   | 调 | tiáo | to adjust | 9 |
|   | 听见 | tīng jiàn | to hear, heard | 3 |
|   | 挺 | tǐng | fairly, quite | 5 |
| W | 碗 | wǎn | bowl | 6 |
|   | 忘记 | wàng jì | to forget | 2 |
|   | 问题 | wèn tí | question, problem | 8 |
|   | 屋 | wū | house, room | 5 |
|   | 午餐 | wǔ cān | lunch | 9 |
| X | 洗手间 | xǐ shǒu jiān | washroom | 3 |
|   | 先生 | xiān sheng | Mr., Sir; husband | 2 |

| | | | | |
|---|---|---|---|---|
| | 相册 | xiàng cè | photo album | 5 |
| | 相片 | xiàng piàn | photograph | 5 |
| | 像 | xiàng | similar to | 5 |
| | 小时 | xiǎo shí | hour | 3 |
| | 行李 | xíng li | luggage | 4 |
| Y | 呀 | ya | [particle signifying emphasis] | 3 |
| | 样子 | yàng zi | appearance, look | 2 |
| | 夜 | yè | night | 9 |
| | 一路上 | yí lù shang | along the way | 1 |
| | 一天到晚 | yì tiān dào wǎn | day to night | 8 |
| | 一下子 | yí xià zi | at once | 4 |
| | 一阵子 | yí zhèn zi | a while | 7 |
| | 姨妈 | yí mā | maternal aunt | 7 |
| | 已经 | yǐ jīng | already | 1 |
| | 以前 | yǐ qián | before | 4 |
| | 以为 | yǐ wéi | to think, to believe, to consider | 8 |
| | 意思 | yì si | meaning | 2 |
| | 游 | yóu | tour, journey | 3 |
| | 与 | yǔ | with | 9 |
| Z | 早 | zǎo | early | 3 |
| | 着急 | zháo jí | to worry | 9 |
| | 这么 | zhè me | such, so | 2 |
| | 这样 | zhè yàng | in this way | 5 |
| | 着 | zhe | [a grammatical word signifying a continued action] | 1 |
| | 正宗 | zhèng zōng | authentic | 9 |
| | 之前 | zhī qián | before | 4 |
| | 只有 | zhǐ yǒu | only | 5 |
| | 中餐 | zhōng cān | Chinese food | 9 |
| | 终于 | zhōng yú | at last, finally | 4 |
| | 主意 | zhǔ yi | idea | 2 |
| | 准备 | zhǔn bèi | to prepare | 1 |
| | 总 | zǒng | always | 8 |
| | 最近 | zuì jìn | recently | 2 |
| | 昨晚 | zuó wǎn | last night | 9 |